A History of
CANADA

A History of
CANADA

Harold Horwood

BISON BOOKS

Published 1983 by Bison Books Corp.
17 Sherwood Place, Greenwich, CT 06830
USA

ISBN 0 86124 090 1

Printed in Hong Kong

PAGE 1: Fur trader Louis Joliet and Jesuit Father Jacques Marquette (standing) explored the Mississippi River.
PREVIOUS PAGE: A fanciful 16th century representation of the arrival in Canada of Jacques Cartier, the French explorer. The map is drawn upside down, with north at the bottom of the page. Florida is in the top right corner, instead of lower left.
THIS PAGE: The time is 9:22 AM, Pacific Coast Time, 7 November 1885. Donald Smith is driving the last spike to allow the first Canadian Pacific railroad train to carry passengers from the Atlantic to the Pacific Ocean.

Contents

The Early Years

The history of Canada begins about the year 1000 when Leif Ericsson, whose father had founded the Norse colony in Greenland, led an expedition to Vinland, and started a series of voyages and colonizing efforts that continued for some 350 years.

Leif was quickly followed by Thorfinn Karlsefni, who brought shiploads of men, women and cattle and founded a settlement at 'Straumfiord', in 1005-6. The Straumfiord settlement was unearthed in 1960, and carbon-dated to the period. It is at L'Anse aux Meadows in northern Newfoundland, and was inhabited for several decades, though not by the original settlers.

The Norse colonies in Canada and Greenland eventually failed, partly because of climatic changes, partly because the modern Inuit moved in from the west and north. The Vikings were followed by Basque whalers, who reached Greenland in 1420, and soon founded stations on Labrador and in northern Newfoundland.

The Portuguese, led by Jao Vaz Cortereal with Norse navigators, reached the same region in 1476. English fishing firms from Bristol were established in Iceland by 1413, and were making direct voyages across the Atlantic to the western fishing grounds by 1480.

We do not know exactly where the Bristol merchants sent their ships, but there is firm evidence that European fishermen were visiting Canada by 1497. In that year John Cabot made his famous voyage looking for a new route to China, and returned with various artifacts picked up on a visit ashore. Among them was a wooden net-needle that could have been left only by a European fishing crew.

Another generation of Cortereals was visiting Canada by 1500, and in 1501 they took a shipload of Indian slaves to Portugal, among them a boy wearing European jewelry, and a man carrying the hilt of a sword made in Italy.

Cabot was a great public relations man, and started a veritable rush to Canada. The English fishing fleets were on the coast by 1498, the French by 1504, the Portuguese and the Spanish by the same period, if not earlier.

The Bristol Company tried to found its first colony in 1503. There is evidence that some men, including Bristol merchants, remained in the colony over the winter, but after a few years it failed, as the Portuguese colony in Cape Breton, founded in 1520, also failed. But the fishery flourished. Before the end of the century there were 10 thousand English fishermen in Newfoundland and perhaps an equal number of French and Basques in Nova Scotia and Labrador.

Disaster was still common. The Basque fleet was frozen in the harbour in the Straits of Belle Isle in 1577, and despite limitless supplies of fish and oil, 540 men died there that winter—probably of scurvy.

Jacques Cartier (1491–1557), the French explorer who discovered the St Lawrence River in 1534 and explored Canada from the Gulf of St Lawrence to what is now Montreal.

Meanwhile the explorers were still busy, and the greatest of them was a sea rover named Jacques Cartier, commissioned by the King of France to find a route to China through the assembly of islands that Canada was still assumed to be. Cartier sailed up the St. Lawrence River, guided by Indians, all the way to Hochelaga, now called Montreal. Given the opportunity, he might have founded a permanent colony, but the French King could not trust the founding of New France to the likes of Cartier, a commoner who might even have been a pirate at one time. He appointed an aristocrat, Jean-François de la Rocque de Roberval to be governor of New France. Roberval, with a shipload of colonists, sailed in 1541. After spending three weeks at St John's he sailed northward around Newfoundland into the Gulf of St. Lawrence. On the way he marooned his pregnant niece, Marguerite, along with her lover and her old servant, on Fogo Island, where she spent two years, surviving conditions that killed her lover, her servant and her baby, before she was rescued by a French fishing ship. The action was typical of Roberval. His colony, at Cap Rouge on the St. Lawrence, was a miserable failure, plagued by executions, deaths from scurvy, and bad relations with the Indians.

Though the colonies with their royal governors failed, the unofficial colonies of fishermen and fur traders succeeded. Fur trading began as an adjunct to fishing. Richard Whitbourne, who spent his working life in Newfoundland, rising from a common sailor in 1579 to become the first Admiralty Court judge in the New World, listed fur trading, along with fishing and whaling, as the object of his first voyage.

French traders established themselves on the lower St. Lawrence, founding the post of Tadoussac, where Indian traders brought furs from the north by way of the Saguenay River, and Canso, on the strait between Nova Scotia and Cape Breton, where Indians from three regions, including New Brunswick, converged annually to trade.

By the end of the 16th century the fur trade was so valuable that the French King saw it as the means of establishing permanent colonies.

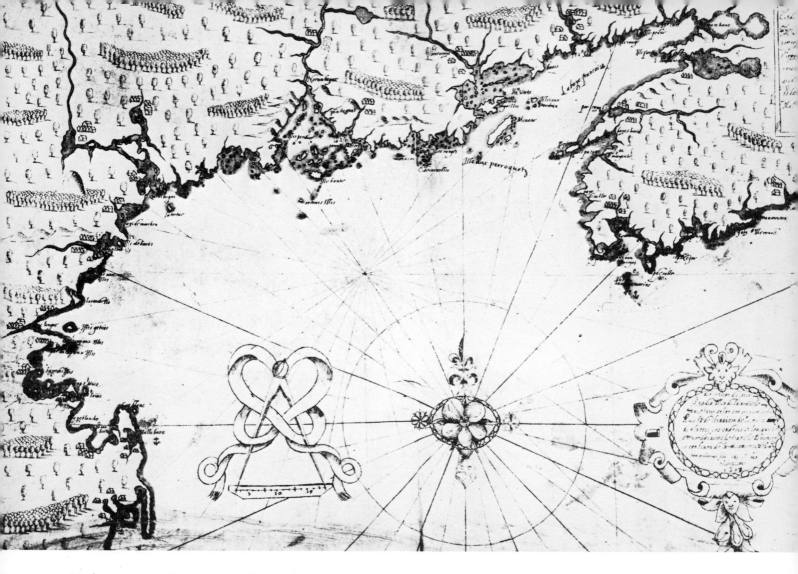

He began granting monopolies to fur traders on condition that they found agricultural colonies at their own expense.

An aristocrat named de Monts with his partner Poutrincourt founded the first such colony at Port Royal, near the estuary of the Annapolis River in Nova Scotia in 1605. European settlement has been continuous there from 1605 to the present. The Annapolis Valley, first cultivated by the Micmac Indians, then by the French, is still one of the best agricultural areas in Canada. It was the first *self-supporting* colony of Europeans in North America. Others— the English in Newfoundland, the French in Quebec—depended on supplies from Europe. The colony of Acadia in Nova Scotia not only survived with no outside help, but flourished. The 300 farmers from northern France who settled in Acadia in the early years of the 17th century, were almost forgotten by the French government, but they increased to a population of 15 thousand in their first century. Just as

Newfoundland was the first successful mercantile colony with an annual trade, measured in today's dollars, in the hundreds of millions, so Nova Scotia was the first successful plantation—a region where a small group of colonists took root and became a native population.

One of the reasons for the success in Nova Scotia was good climate and good soil. Another was good peasant stock, from Normandy and Brittany. A third was good relations with the Indians; French and Micmacs in Nova Scotia co-operated and intermarried, and were allies against the English who, from an early date, raided the colony, and eventually took it over.

De Monts and Poutrincourt both returned to France, but only after Poutrincourt had bankrupted himself getting the colony started. His son, Jean de Biencourt, remained in Nova Scotia, started a family, and lived there all his life.

At Port Royal Poutrincourt founded The Order of Good Cheer, a dining club whose members took turns providing weekly feasts. From all accounts they ate well: moose meat, beaver tail, lobster, geese, and a great variety of local vegetables. They raised wheat and rye and built a grist mill which amazed the Indians by its cleverness—they had never thought of getting a river to work for them.

Much of this first successful colony is still visible. The houses and fort have been rebuilt on their original foundations. The grist mill (now producing electricity instead of meal) has been reconstructed on the mountain river where it was founded in 1606. Even the Order of Good Cheer still exists at Annapolis Royal, the modern successor to the first French town in Canada.

While the Acadian farmers flourished peacefully, the fur trade flourished violently. Its center moved from Nova Scotia to what is now New Brunswick, and there, on Easter Sunday, 1645, the fur trading colony founded by Poutrincourt's son, Charles de Biencourt, was attacked by a rival fur trader Charles d'Aulnay, who, after accepting the surrender of the colonists with a promise of safe conduct, proceeded to hang them from the rafters of their fort.

Violence continued to be a tradition of the fur trade for the next three centuries. It produced, among many atrocities, the massacre of the Huron nation by the Iroquois, and finally, the bloody battles between the Hudson's Bay Company and the Northwest Company, when the trade reached its culmination in northern Saskatchewan and among the foothills of the Rocky Mountains.

But in the early years of the 17th century the fur trade was still in its infancy. The great crop in early Canada (as in the early New England colonies) was fish. Nothing to rival the fishery appeared before the founding of the Virginia tobacco plantations. Because of their sea power, established by the defeat of the Spanish Armada, followed by the success of such privateers as Drake, Raleigh and Easton, the English were paramount at sea and in the fishery.

The principal challenge to the English fishery came not from other countries, but from pirates. Fish cargoes were hijacked at sea, much as cargoes of whiskey were hijacked during Prohibition. Captain Whitbourne lost one such

OPPOSITE PAGE: Champlain's map of the Canadian coast, executed in 1607. Champlain was the founder of Quebec.

ABOVE: English fishing fleets were working off the coast of Newfoundland as early as the 16th century.

cargo that he valued (in today's money) at $100,000.

The most famous of the pirates, Peter Easton, has a monument erected to his memory at Harbour Grace in Newfoundland, the port that he first fortified, and later recaptured from the French. Easton was not just a pirate captain, but a pirate *admiral,* who commanded whole fleets of ships, and enlisted more than 500 Newfoundland fishermen into his crews. Easton crowned his career by capturing a fleet of Spanish treasure ships in mid-Atlantic in 1614, after which he retired to the French Riviera with a vast fortune and became Marquis of Savoy.

He was followed by Henry Mainwarring, whose career was almost as spectacular. Mainwarring, already a navigator and member of the English bar at the age of 23, was commissioned by the British Admiralty to sail in pursuit of Easton. Missing the chance to capture Easton, he sailed off to capture Spanish ships instead, made his base in Newfoundland, using Easton's old fort at Harbour Grace, and grew so enormously wealthy that King James was more than pleased to offer him a 'free' pardon on condition that he come home, share his wealth, and make his experience available to the government.

This Mainwarring did. He was pardoned, knighted, and elected to Parliament, became Vice-Admiral of the British fleet, published a famous book on seamanship, and organized a campaign against piracy that virtually drove the pirates from the high seas for a generation.

Samuel de Champlain, the founder of French Canada, depicted in a 19th century oil painting by Theophile Hamel.

After Mainwarring's time there were periods when either England or France had enough sea power to police the North Atlantic, but early in the 18th century chaos returned, and the Atlantic coast of Canada was plagued by pirates big and small for almost fifty years.

One of the briefest and bloodiest careers was that of John Phillips, a Newfoundland shipbuilder who, with five companions, stole a New England fishing vessel at St. Peters in 1723, and for the next eight months terrorized the Atlantic, capturing at least 33 ships, some of them armed, and one actually a 12-gun sloop-of-war.

In April 1724 Phillips was finally overpow-

ered by Andrew Harridan, a Boston fishing captain. Ten of the pirates were 'thrown to the sharks', several others were chained and taken ashore for trial, and Harridan sailed into Boston with Phillips' head hanging as a trophy from his yardarm.

But the darkest pair of criminals of this period were Edward Cobham and Maria Lindsay, who preyed on supply ships and cargoes of furs in the Gulf of St Lawrence from 1720 to 1740. They went completely undetected, because they murdered every man, woman or child who fell into their hands, and sank every ship, selling their cargoes on the Mediterranean black market.

Then they retired to France, bought an estate, and bought their way into the aristocracy. Cobham was even appointed a magistrate. His piracies would never have been known had he not confessed them on his death bed, and asked to have the story published. Despite attempts by his family to suppress it, it survives, today, in fragments, in the French archives.

Not all the pirates are remembered as monsters. Some of them, such as Easton, are revered as Canadian folk heroes, somewhat in the tradition of Robin Hood. Most of their crewmen were volunteers. They offered sailors an alternative to the near-slavery of the fishing plantations, a chance at something like real independence, and something more than a starvation wage.

The principal legacy of the era of piracy is found today in Newfoundland's picturesque place names. Happy Adventure was named for a pirate ship. So was Heart's Desire. Black Joke Cove was named for a famous American privateer—the Black Joke. We might go on and on through a score of such names, each of them chosen by some free spirit of a former century for the ship in which he sought fulfillment of his hopes and dreams.

Though the English fishing stations in Newfoundland were several times destroyed by French raids, England's hold on the colony was never really broken. It was the one part of Canada that remained in English hands throughout the long struggle between the two great colonial powers, when, for a time, it seemed that most of North America might become incorpo-

View of a Stage & also of ȳ manner of Fishing for, Curing & Drying Cod at NEW FOUND LAND.

.The Habit of ȳ Fishermen. B. The Line. C. The manner of Fishing. D. The Dreſſers of ȳ Fiſh. E. The Trough into
ch they throw ȳ Cod when Dreſſed. F. Salt Boxes. G. The manner of Carrying ȳ Cod. H. The Cleanſing ȳ Cod. I. A Preſs
ttract ȳ Oyl from ȳ Cods Livers. R: Casks to receive ȳ Water & Blood that comes from ȳ Livers. L. Another Cask to receive
Oyl. M. The manner of Drying ȳ Cod.

Fishermen are drying codfish in Newfoundland, a fertile port of call for pirates, in this 1715 engraving. The pirates would raid the cargo-laden merchant ships and often found recruits among the local fishermen.

rated into the great empire of New France, whose centre of government, trade, and spiritual sway was the fortress of Quebec, built on a great rock overlooking the St. Lawrence River, a thousand miles from the open sea.

Samuel Champlain, who founded Quebec, had been a map maker with de Monts and Poutrincourt when they founded Port Royal. A man of humble origins, son of a naval officer, he was later to become Governor of New France and to insert the aristocratic 'de' between Samuel and Champlain.

Unlike the earlier colonies in Newfoundland and Nova Scotia, which flourished on fishing and farming, and only marginally on furs, the colony at Quebec was founded squarely on the fur trade, and the empire of New France, of which it was the centre, was really one vast trading post, bartering cheap hardware and cheaper liquor from Europe and the West Indies, for beaver and ermine and sable and fox.

When Champlain landed at Quebec in 1608 he was still acting as agent for de Monts, who still hoped to make his fortune in the fur trade. He discovered, shortly after landing, that some of his men were plotting to kill him and turn the operation over to de Monts' competitors. Champlain suppressed this rebellion by hanging its leader, sending three others back to France, and pardoning the rest. This seems to

Fr Isaac Jogues, a French Jesuit, is shown being attacked by the Iroquois in 1642. He was later ransomed by the Dutch, then murdered by the Mohawks.

It was a grave error of judgement. The Iroquois were anxious for peaceful trade with the French. They had formed a federation of tribes whose avowed aim was universal peace. They were middlemen, already advanced in the arts of trade and diplomacy, depending largely on their relations with distant tribes, and anxious to build up a trading empire reaching into the west and north. The French, by allying themselves with the primitive hunting tribes north of the St Lawrence River, and joining in their raids against the Iroquois, set the seal of doom on the French empire in Canada. They later developed the Hurons into a competing force for the Iroquois fur trade, and provoked the great war in which the Huron nation was destroyed.

While Champlain's judgment was often at fault, his energy was always admirable. In 1615 he travelled with the Indians along the shore of Lake Ontario to the Trent River, up the Trent and its neighbouring waterways to Georgian Bay on Lake Huron, then southward, and across Lake Ontario where he and his Huron companions were defeated in an attack on an Iroquois village. He spent 18 years on such travels, exploring most of what is now eastern Canada, and managing to keep enough furs moving into Quebec to stave off total bankruptcy.

But New France was never more than a trading bridgehead on a continent dominated by enemies. By 1627 the population of Champlain's colony was 107. To the east and south were the English colonies of Newfoundland and New England, with 2110 planters, reinforced in the summer with 4000 fishermen. To the southwest were the Iroquois.

In 1628 David Kirke, later governor of Newfoundland, decided that Quebec was a plum ripe for the plucking. With his four brothers, each captain of a ship, he sailed up the St Lawrence, occupied the French fur trading post of Tadoussac, captured the supply fleet sent to Champlain from France, and next spring received the surrender of the capital of New France without having had to fire a shot.

The Kirkes sent Champlain and his colonists home to France and took over their fur trade. Kirke remained in charge of the former French colony until 1633, when, under treaty with En-

have established his authority, but by no means ended his problems. Only eight of the original 28 colonists survived the first winter.

But with spring came supplies and more colonists from France. Champlain, meanwhile, had made an alliance with the Montagnais Indians against the Iroquois, and joined a war party on which he discovered Lake Champlain. Next year he led another war party which wiped out an Iroquois settlement on the Richelieu River. These were the beginnings of Champlain's extensive travels in the New World, and also the beginning of the disastrous enmity between the French settlers and the Iroquois, the most powerful, and most politically advanced people in the region claimed by the French King.

gland, Champlain and his colonists were allowed to return. Champlain died at Quebec in 1635. He had truly devoted his life to Canada, but did not live to see his work bear fruit. At his death the empire of New France still looked like a pipe dream.

Just then, however, real settlers, accompanied by wives, children and servants, began to arrive at Quebec for the first time. By 1641 approximately 200 of them had taken up farming and trades in the St Lawrence Valley. In that year, too, new colonists inspired by religious and social plans, arrived—among them the founders of Montreal—at first just an outpost in the far wilderness, but soon to become the greatest centre of the fur trade in North America, and in time to grow to one of the two largest cities in the future nation of Canada.

The Kirkes, meanwhile, retired to Newfoundland, and began a flourishing plantation in the little settlement of Ferryland, where Lord Baltimore, who also founded the colony of Maryland, had preceded them. David Kirke was Newfoundland's first royal governor, with authority over the whole island. He ruled a ribald band of fishermen, nearly all of them illiterate, and with no knowledge of law, order or religion. His principal perquisite as governor was the sale of rum, and he opened a tavern in every port.

At Quebec, authority was more explicit, and the Church, with its hospitals and schools, was a powerful force. Indeed, the most powerful individual at Quebec, after Champlain, was the Mother Superior of the Ursuline convent, Marie of the Incarnation. Governors and bishops came to her for advice. She ran both a hospital and a school. Her friend Madame de la Peltrie, an enormously wealthy heiress, also emigrated to Quebec as patroness of the Ursuline order and spent her fortune on building up the colony.

A third woman, Jeanne Manse, was co-founder, with Paul Chomdey de Maisonneuve, of Montreal, and did more than even the governor to keep the colony alive. She had powerful friends in France from whom she was able to secure money and troops to buy supplies and fight off the frequent attacks of the Iroquois. But the survival of Montreal, surrounded by

The Royal Charter of 1670 founding the Hudson's Bay Company. The company was to locate the Northwest Passage, promote settlement and do business in the region.

hostile Iroquois, was only due in small measure to the handful of soldiers who defended it. Far more important was the almost superstitious awe in which the French were held by the Indians. This awe, beginning with the exploits of Champlain and the tiny band of *coureurs de bois* that he sent among the Indians, was strengthened by the Jesuit priests who went among the Hurons, were captured by their enemies the Iroquois, and died at the stake under prolonged torture with such superhuman courage that the Indians ate their hearts—the supreme tribute to a dead enemy.

The awe was strengthened further when a band of 17 French soldiers at the Long Sault, upriver from Montreal, was besieged in a tiny improvised fort by hundreds of Iroquois warriors, and held out for a week, taking a dreadful toll of the attackers. Such acts of lonely courage—Father Isaac Jogues, who returned to the Iroquois to be martyred after having previously been tortured and mutilated; Father Brebeuf, who gave praise to God while the red-hot axe heads burnt their way into his flesh; soldiers who fought at their best when outnumbered a hundred to one—inspired such superstitious dread among their enemies that they failed to attack Quebec and Montreal at a time when they could easily have destroyed both and thus ended the French incursion. By the time Jeanne

Manse died at Montreal in 1673, the town she had helped to found had a population of 1500, and New France was beyond the power of the Iroquois to destroy. Its real test would come later in a struggle with the colonies founded by the English to the south and east, supported by English arms from overseas.

For almost a century New France flourished. Quebec became the centre of an empire that included Montreal and trading posts far to the west, on the Great Lakes, the distant farm and fishing colony of Acadia, and the even more distant fishing ports of southern Newfoundland, dominated by the great fortress of Placentia, where a governor drawing his authority from Quebec ruled the French fisheries of the western Atlantic and policed a trade that extended between Montreal and the Caribbean.

Though Quebec was the capital, Montreal was the chief commercial town of this empire. Eight hundred canoe loads of Indians and *coureurs de bois* arrived there annually for the

The landing of the British New England forces during the taking of Louisbourg on Cape Breton Island off the northeast coast of Nova Scotia in 1745. The fortress fell and was occupied by New England militiamen.

Sun King, Louis XIV of France. Talon not only started a successful program of economic development (farming, lumber milling, shipbuilding, iron working, brick making, and many small industries) but also set out to build up the population by finding wives for every sailor, adventurer or ex-soldier who wanted to settle in the colony.

His scheme was to bring out from France orphan girls, who were already wards of the government, and any other girls who would volunteer, and to marry them off in one great ceremony, on arrival, to the waiting bachelors. It worked. The 'King's Daughters', as they were called, arrived by the hundreds each year between 1665 and 1671; more than 1100 in all were married, settled on land, and within a year most were raising children. The birthrate soared to the point where the population doubled every six years.

But in spite of all these schemes, it was the fur trade that kept New France alive, that produced its export revenues, its government taxes, and the wealth of its merchants. The trade, in turn, depended on the *coureurs de bois,* who travelled deep into the woods, along canoe routes that they learned from the Indians, and brought home the furs that the Indians had collected from places even further away. In exchange for furs they traded brandy (later West Indian rum), cloth, and such hardware as traps, needles and knives.

Strangely enough, the *coureurs* were outlaws. They led lives proscribed by church and state. None of them had a license to travel or trade, and if brought before a court they could, in theory, be imprisoned, flogged, or hanged for their activities. Despite this they flourished, because the colony could not collect furs by any other means. After the Hurons were defeated and absorbed by the Iroquois in the great Indian war, there were no Indian middlemen capable of making fur trading trips into the interior of the continent. So young Frenchmen, successors to those trained by Champlain, took up the work, making long and hazardous canoe trips of 1000 to 1500 miles inland, returning after six months' absence half starved and half naked, but with boatloads of furs that made them temporarily rich. The money quickly van-

greatest fur market in the world, and its explorers, the *coureurs,* pushed westward until they came within sight of the foothills of the Rocky Mountains. They even reached the Mississippi River, travelled down its course to the Gulf of Mexico, and there founded the colony of Louisiana, so completing the encirclement of the flourishing English colonies that later became the United States of America.

The greatest civilian builder of New France was the intendant Jean Talon appointed by the

ished, spent on liquor and women, but the furs remained, to enrich the colony, while the *coureurs* headed back to the woods for more of the same. When French authorities brought them before a court, the provincial judges refused to enforce the harsh laws, but fined them and turned them loose to continue their essential trade. In fact, the entire colony conspired to protect the outlaws.

Meanwhile the English had entered the Canadian fur trade in force by organizing the Hudson's Bay Company under Prince Rupert, cousin of King Charles II of England. The prince was made governor of Rupert's Land, which the English defined as all the lands on rivers draining into the Arctic, the Pacific, and the Mississippi (most of the North American Continent) and under his patronage fur trading posts were built in Hudson's Bay on the estuaries of great rivers down which the Indians could bring furs in perfect safety, unmolested by the Iroquois or any other hostile people.

The Hudson's Bay Company moved slowly inland along these rivers, and gradually won the struggle for the west, though not before French explorers had opened trading posts on the prairies as far west as the Saskatchewan River.

The fall of New France was inevitable. By the middle of the eighteenth century its vast territory stretching from Newfoundland to Saskatchewan, and from the Gulf of Mexico almost to the Arctic, was held by a mere 60 thousand people, facing an English colonial population of more than a million.

Despite being always outnumbered, the French scored brilliant victories. They attacked and destroyed the English settlements in Newfoundland, but had no troops to garrison their conquests. They moved on, and the English soon returned. They destroyed the English trading posts in Hudson's Bay, but there the same thing happened. They lacked the manpower to keep the territory won by such brilliant leaders as Pierre le Moyne d'Iberville.

When the last struggle with England began, the English held the entire Atlantic coast, except for Cape Breton Island with its great French fort of Louisbourg, at the entrance to the St Lawrence waterway, and even Louis-bourg was not, in fact, defensible. It had been captured with little difficulty by a New England expedition in 1745, but restored to France in the subsequent peace treaty. Though difficult to attack from the sea, it was vulnerable to attack by land.

Louisbourg had to be held, and the St Lawrence kept open to French shipping, bringing troops and supplies from France, in any war with England—otherwise, Quebec and Montreal could be isolated and forced to surrender. This was the situation in 1755 when the last struggle for Canada began.

In that year George Washington led a troop of Indians and Virginians to the Ohio to stake a claim to that part of the territory claimed by New France. They met and defeated a French Canadian party whose commander was killed and scalped after he had begun to retreat—an action that so incensed the French that they sent a strong detachment of troops after Washington, caught him, besieged him, and forced him to sign a capitulation promising to stay out of Ohio territory for a year.

But the war was on. The English sent troops under General Braddock to Virginia, reinforced their garrisons in Nova Scotia and Newfoundland, and began expelling the French settlers from Acadia, scattering some of them through English colonies from the Caribbean to Labrador, and shipping others to France. (Many of these expelled farmers later returned, and became ancestors to the large Acadian population that lives in Nova Scotia today.)

The centre of English power was at Halifax, the strongest fortress in the world outside Europe, but England's principal interest in what is now Canada still lay in Newfoundland, where the colonial and floating population produced 70 million pounds of dried fish annually, one of the mainstays of the English economy. There were forts at St John's, Ferryland, Placentia and Trinity.

General Braddock was the first of several incompetents sent out by the English as colonial commanders. He was killed in his first battle with the French general, the Marquis de Montcalm, a commander with a great reputation, who managed to win battle after battle against armies much larger than his own. But in time,

An etching of 1759, *Quebec, the Capital of New-France, a Bishoprick and Seat of the Soverain Court.* The cathedral is the building with the tallest spire.

numbers began to prevail.

General Amherst, sent to capture Louisbourg, besieged a garrison of 6000 troops with an army of 27,000, supported by 35 to 40 British warships. After a seven week siege, Louisbourg fell on 26 July 1758, and New France was doomed. The English should now have sealed the St Lawrence with their superior naval forces and starved New France into submission. That was the easy course that the cautious General Amherst would have chosen.

Instead, the British allowed an entire French fleet to sail up the St Lawrence to reinforce Quebec for the next spring, while they prepared three armies to take the famous fortress by storm. The principal assault was in command of the dashing General Wolfe, who led 9000 troops up the St Lawrence in ships. An army of 6000 advanced under Amherst by way of Lake Champlain, and a third army from New England captured the French fort of Niagara.

While waiting for the arrival of his reinforcing armies, Wolfe devastated the St Lawrence valley, ranging up and down both banks of the river burning every Canadian farm as he went. He also hammered the buildings of Quebec into rubble by artillery fire. Though the outer defences of the town remained intact, 80 percent of its houses and public buildings were ruined.

The reinforcements never did arrive, and Wolfe finally decided on a surprise attack, scaling a narrow cliff path by night, and planting his army on the Plains of Abraham, close to the city gates, at dawn.

Faced with this sudden emergency, Montcalm made his one fatal mistake. Instead of waiting some hours to collect the strongest French force possible (a force that would have been decidedly superior to Wolfe's) he rushed out to battle with the Quebec garrison. It was over in 15 minutes, with the French fleeing back inside the walls of the city, and both Wolfe and Montcalm dying of bullet wounds. With his dying breath, Montcalm made one last error. Instead of ordering the gates closed against the attackers, he ordered the city to be surrendered to the English.

That did not end the war. The French regrouped their armies, and the next spring attacked and defeated the English at the second

The Death of General Wolfe by the American artist Benjamin West. Both the British commander, Gen James Wolfe, and the French field marshal, the Marquis Louis Joseph de Montcalm, were killed in the Battle of Quebec.

battle of Quebec. But the English did what the French should have done the year before. They fled inside the town, closed its gates, and withstood a siege until a fleet arrived and dispersed the attackers. Montreal, faced that year with three armies of overwhelming superiority, surrendered without a fight.

But the French still had not lost Canada. A war, like a game of chess, can sometimes be won by a surprise move from an inferior position. With Quebec lost, and the war between France and England on a worldwide basis dragging to its end, the French made a master stroke. They sent a small army to capture the English forts in Newfoundland. If they could hold Newfoundland until the peace conference, Britain would almost certainly agree to restore Quebec to France in exchange. Quebec was of little interest to England, whose fur trade was already flourishing further north, but the Newfoundland fishery was vital.

The French expeditionary force did not succeed fully. It captured St John's and rebuilt the fortifications to withstand a siege, but it failed to take the forts at Ferryland and Placentia, which were reinforced just in time.

The recapture of St John's by the British was a textbook battle, the one truly outstanding bit of tactical brilliance of the war for Canada. Led by Colonel Amherst, a force of Scots, Swiss and German mercenaries landed at Torbay north of St John's, marched southward and took Quidi Vidi in a short battle, then, three days later, in a dense fog and the black of night, crept up Signal Hill, took the French fort there by surprise, and trained its guns on the larger fort in the town, which held the main French garrison, and which could not reply to gunfire from the hill. Amherst then sent a message to the French commander, pointing out that he was completely out-manoeuvred, and threatening that, if he did not surrender, every man in the fort would be put to the sword.

So St John's was recaptured almost without bloodshed, and the French Fleur-de-lis came down over the last town held by France in Canada.

The Expansion

That Canada remained British during and after the American War of Independence seems like one of the marvels of history, especially if we think of 'Canada' traditionally as a colonial French country ruled by a few hundred British troops and their camp followers.

The truth is far more complex. First of all, the country that was to become Canada included, besides Quebec and a west populated only by Indians, the Atlantic colonies that were later to become four provinces, and those colonies, in 1760, had a population of 28,000, mainly of English origin, as partial balance to the 60,000 French Canadians.

The view of Canada as a French-speaking colony gradually expanded by later waves of English-speaking immigrants is a simplistic, Ontario-centered view that regards the eastern provinces as mere appendages. Canada from its beginnings was as bi-lingual and bi-cultural as it is today.

Equally important: in the years between the fall of New France (1763) and the Boston Tea Party (1773) Britain had taken on the role of protector of the French Canadian settlers against traders and land grabbers from other parts of British North America who swarmed into Quebec after the conquest, determined upon looting a conquered country.

James Murray, the first British governor of Quebec, did what he could to protect the rights of the inhabitants against this swarm of locusts. His finest achievement was the Quebec Act of 1774, which confirmed his policy of preserving Quebec civil law, and with it the property rights of the *Quebecois*, though British criminal law replaced the criminal law of France. The Quebec Act also guaranteed freedom to practice the Roman Catholic religion.

The immigrant British colonials had managed to corner the trade and commerce of Quebec, but they failed to seize its houses and lands, as they had hoped. They mounted a campaign to get rid of Murray, and succeeded, but he was replaced by Carleton, who turned out to be just as sympathetic to the French, and an even abler leader.

When the American War of Independence began, there were republican sympathizers in Canada—mainly in Nova Scotia, which had been settled mostly by New Englanders—but very few in Quebec. To the amazement of the Americans, the recently conquered *Canadiens* remained loyal to their British rulers, as did the powerful Iroquois confederacy and the Newfoundland colony. Newfoundland sent a regiment to defend Quebec City, and the Bishop of Quebec ordered the rites of the church to be denied to any Catholic who joined the revolt.

The war in Canada began in 1775. Governor Carleton regarded Montreal as indefensible, and ordered it evacuated. American troops occupied it without resistance. But their attack on Quebec, 31 December 1775, was a disaster. Carleton proved to be a brilliant commander. He lost only six men in the battle. The Americans lost 400 prisoners and 220 killed, among them General Montgomery. The Americans retreated in disorder, abandoning many of their arms. The Indians and *habitants* might easily have turned the retreat into a massacre, but Carleton, a humane man, ordered the fleeing army to be allowed to go unmolested.

The Americans won their war elsewhere. In Canada, the effect was twofold. First, it established a separate Canadian identity, and sketched the future border with the United States from the Great Lakes to the sea. Second, it brought a flood of refugees, 50 thousand British Empire Loyalists from the 13 American colonies, who altered the balance of the population in Canada.

The Loyalists, offered grants of Crown land in Canada, practically created the new provinces of New Brunswick and Ontario, strongly reinforced the English settlers in Nova Scotia, and created the large English-speaking minority in the province of Quebec.

Before their arrival, New Brunswick had

A group of Loyalists camping on the banks of the St Lawrence, 6 June 1784. INSET: Governor James Murray of Quebec.

been Nova Scotia's 'wild west,' inhabited by Indians and bush rangers. The Loyalists founded the city of St John, the first incorporated city of Canada, granted a Royal Charter in 1785, and made it one of the greatest shipbuilding and mercantile ports of the 19th century.

Before their arrival, Ontario had been Quebec's 'wild west,' the preserve of explorers and fur traders. From Niagara to Lake St Francis on the St Lawrence River, they turned it into thriving farm land and towns filled with industrial crafts—mills, forges, brick works, potteries and lumber yards.

Meanwhile there were notable developments in other places. In 1770 Samuel Hearne began his expedition from Hudson Bay to the Coppermine River, becoming the first white man to reach the Arctic Ocean overland. Moravian missionaries, under government protection, set up posts in Labrador and ended the guerrilla warfare between the Inuit and the white fishermen. Dr Lynch at Trinity, Newfoundland introduced smallpox vaccination to North America only two years after it was successfully tested by Edward Jenner in England. At the other end of the country, James Cook explored Nootka

Sound and claimed British Columbia for England. Eleven years after Cook, Alexander Mackenzie and his *voyageurs* from Montreal reached the Arctic ocean at the mouth of the Mackenzie River, near the present border with Alaska. Two years later, in 1791, Mackenzie was leader of the first expedition to cross Canada to the Pacific. He beat Lewis and Clark by 12 years.

That same year, slavery was abolished in British North America, and Canada soon became the Promised Land for escaping American slaves.

A census of 1790 had placed the population of Canada at 161,311. But this is deceptive. The figure does not include the Atlantic Provinces, the Arctic, or the Indian population of north and west. Next year Quebec was divided into Upper and Lower Canada. Upper Canada's legislature first met at Newark (Niagara-on-the-Lake) but in 1793 moved to York (Toronto). The capital of Lower Canada remained where it always had been—Quebec City. The next year Britain finally signed a treaty of 'amity, commerce and navigation' with the United States, the border was recognized, and friendly trade between Canada and her southern neighbour began—it was not to last long.

The USS *Constitution*, known as 'Old Ironsides,' rakes the crippled *Guerriere* off Nova Scotia, 19 August 1812.

The closing years of the 18th century were a period of rapid demoralization for Canada's Indians. The conquest of Quebec had been followed immediately by Chief Pontiac's war, a bloody series of raids and sieges carried out by the Ottawa Indians and their allies against the British. Some 500 soldiers and 2000 settlers were killed before Pontiac buried the hatchet, accepting the inevitable after three years of fighting. Despite this, and similar, though less effective 'rebellions' by Indians defending their homelands, the tide of white settlement rolled westward. Before the end of the century, white settlers were firmly entrenched along the shores of the Great Lakes and their connecting rivers, all the way to Lake Superior, and the first canal had been built at Sault Ste Marie, to enable ships to reach the lakehead.

Western tribes such as the Ojibway and the Sioux were now within the Canadian orbit, and the Ojibway were getting guns from the British to equalize their struggle with their more powerful neighbours to the west.

The gun trade was perhaps the greatest disaster for the Indians. Guns not only made tribal wars more deadly, but made it possible to ex-terminate the game, and with it the Indian way of life. At the same time, tuberculosis, smallpox and alcoholism swept through the tribes, wiping out entire bands, and so demoralizing the survivors that they often became mere scavengers picking through the scraps and bones scattered by the white man's march across the continent.

The fur trade flourished mightily in this same period. Savage competition between the Hudson's Bay Company and the North West Company (the latter based at Montreal) led men to the Arctic and the Pacific, created a network of trade routes, and established competing posts far inland, often well provisioned and well armed, for the competition was by no means peaceful. The price of beaver pelts soared 100 percent, but the Indians benefitted little, because most of the payment was in rum from the Hudson's Bay Company, or rum and whiskey from the North Westers. The latter were the great explorers, first to travel across the continent by canoe, first to go down the great Mackenzie River to the Beaufort Sea, first to explore the Rocky Mountain passes and the great rivers that flow through their trenches.

But they took such a toll of furs as they went that their older, better-organized competitors had to follow hard on their heels.

The North West trading expeditions were headed by hard-bitten Scots who had come to Canada to wring wealth from the wilderness, but they were manned almost exclusively by French Canadian canoemen, *voyageurs,* direct descendants from the *coureurs de bois* who had taken the flag of New France to the Great Plains and the Gulf of Mexico. The *voyageurs* accomplished incredible feats of endurance, taking their loaded canoes up-river, against the current and past rapids, as much as 50 or 60 miles a day, including sometimes as many as a dozen portages.

In the fur trade, the dream of rags-to-riches sometimes came true. Simon McTavish, a barefoot Scottish immigrant at 13, became first an apprentice, then an independent trader, then founder of the North West coalition, and died in 1804 the richest man in Canada.

Such famous explorers as Alexander Mackenzie, Simon Fraser, and David Thompson, who established the routes to the Pacific and gave their names to the great rivers, were all North Westers.

The Hudson's Bay Company, which followed them, and eventually swallowed them, lamented that it was forced by the North Westers to trade in rum. Sir George Simpson, most famous of the HBC governors, who himself made a voyage across the continent, reported that as much as 20,000 gallons of spirits were traded annually.

Wherever they went, the fur traders took Indian wives (usually more than one) and fathered children. Simpson himself sired seven, and the North West Company, before its merger with the HBC, was supporting six hundred children at its posts.

After the American border was drawn at the Pigeon River on the western shore of Lake Superior, the fur traders built Fort William in Thunder Bay as the point where western furs would be trans-shipped to Montreal. From that point the fur route stretched westward through a maze of lakes and rivers to the Upper Churchill in what is now Northern Saskatchewan, and thence over a steep divide into rivers

The death of the Shawnee chief Tecumseh at the Battle of the River Thames, October 1813. Lithograph by Currier and Ives.

flowing westward into the Rocky Mountains. It was a long and difficult route by which to supply the trading posts, and ship out the furs, but the profits were well worth it. For every thousand dollars worth of supplies shipped westward, three or four thousand dollars worth of furs came back—almost without exception the major traders grew wealthy, and spent their wealth on the status symbols of the day: mansions, coaches, servants and expensive living.

Nothing halted the fur trade. It went on during the three years of Pontiac's War, the eight years of the American War of Independence, and the three years when Canada fought for her life in the War of 1812.

In some ways, that war is the central fact of Canadian history. It might be called Canada's War of Independence, for though it did not establish independence from Great Britain—that came much more slowly—it established Canada's independence from the United States. American history gives various reasons for the conflict: a dispute over trade or the impressment of Americans into the British navy; but the central cause of the war was simply the American desire to unite the whole continent under the Stars and Stripes.

While Britain was occupied with Napoleon in Europe, Canada looked like an easy prize. Its conquest, according to President Jefferson, would be a mere matter of marching. Secretary of War William Eustis concurred: 'We can take Canada without soldiers. We have only to send officers. . . .'

Except for General Isaac Brock, it might have been almost that easy. There was a strong sense of defeatism in Ontario, and quite a few sympathizers for the republican cause. The defense of Canada, a nation of half a million facing one of seven and a half million, seemed hopeless. Brock could muster only 5,000 troops, most of them in Nova Scotia and Quebec. West of Montreal he had only 1500 regulars.

BOTTOM: The Battle of Queenston, 13 October 1812.
BELOW: Maj Gen. Sir Isaac Brock.

Brock was governor of Upper Canada when the United States declared war. Finding the legislature half-hearted about defence, he dissolved it, took the government into his own hands, and ordered immediate mobilization. Next he ordered an attack from the remote and unlikely post of Sault Ste Marie, west of Lake Huron. Forty-five regulars, 180 militiamen, and some 400 Indians descended upon the American fort at Mackinac Island, about 50 miles inside the border. Taken completely by surprise, the garrison surrendered. The victorious invaders then rushed southward and took Fort Dearborn (Chicago). The retreating column of Americans, including two women and twelve children, was attacked by local Indians and massacred.

Meanwhile Brock, in a counter-attack against Brigadier General William Hull, who had invaded Canada from Detroit, captured Fort Detroit, and with it enough arms and ammunition to supply an army twice the size of his own. He took over 2000 prisoners, including the American general.

Brock's final hour of glory came on 13 October 1812, when he attacked and defeated the American force that had crossed the Niagara River at Queenston Heights. Out of an American army of 6300, only 1600 landed on the Canadian side, and of these, 1250 were killed, wounded, or taken prisoner, against a Cana-

ABOVE: York (Toronto) being attacked by Americans, 27 April 1813.
BELOW: A representation of the capture of the city of Washington by the British forces in 1814.

dian loss of 14 men killed and 73 wounded. Among the Canadian dead was General Brock, who had been killed by an American marksman in the first charge.

But in three and a half months Brock had rallied Canada to the British cause, secured the west, consolidated the Niagara Peninsula, and proved that small, spirited armies, could defeat larger, badly led masses of ill-trained troops.

The following year, an American invasion force of 4000 under Major General Wade Hampton was routed by 800 French Canadians under Charles Michel de Salaberry at the battle of Chateauguay, near Montreal. The Americans were incredulous that the French Canadians would fight 'for the British.' What they didn't understand was that they were fighting for Canada, on soil owned by their ancestors for the past two centuries. A second American invasion force of 8,000 also failed to take Montreal that year, and retreated with substantial losses of men and equipment.

Not all the battles were won by the defenders. In southwestern Ontario, Canada was defended largely by Indian soldiers, fighting under the great Shawnee chief Tecumseh. He was killed at the Battle of the Thames in October 1813, and Canadian forces were pushed out of the southwest as far as Fort Erie and the shores of Lake Ontario. The Americans won command of Lake Erie, and raided, with impunity, along the shore.

In the late stages of the war, arson ran rampant. The Americans burned York (Toronto) and Newark (Niagara-on-the-Lake). In reprisal for the destruction of Newark, the Canadians burned every town, village and hamlet from Buffalo to Niagara Falls.

The last major battle for Upper Canada was fought on the southwestern tip of the Niagara Peninsula on 25 July 1814. In the Battle of Lundy's Lane, 3500 seasoned American troops clashed with an equal number of British and Canadians, and were decisively defeated. When the war ended, as it did on 24 December, 1814, the only Americans on Canadian soil were a small detachment dug in near Amherstburg.

For Americans, the War of 1812 is remembered as a successful defiance of the British lion. For Canadians it was much more crucial, the beginning of their nationhood, a war in which British, French and Indians had stood together and defeated a foreign invader. The sense of national unity so created was soon to be put to severe stress.

It took two or three generations to heal the wounds of the War of 1812. The memory of farms and villages and towns looted and burned along a thousand miles of the border faded slowly, and caused Canadians to turn eastward toward Britain rather than southward toward the United States as their principal friend and ally.

In this period Canada, like her neighbour, became preoccupied with 'the opening of the west'—that is to say, with stealing the land from the Indians and the descendants of the *voyageurs* who had been born there. The Indians had fought as hard as the Canadians to preserve their independence, and had been promised by Britain that a separate Indian nation would be established, but in the peace treaty the Indians were abandoned.

Then, in 1815, the Red River Settlement was established by Lord Selkirk, as a home for Scottish Highlanders who had been evicted from their own lands. Selkirk, head of the Hudson's Bay Company, was the natural enemy of the North West fur traders, who in turn were the natural allies of the Indians and the *Metis*, the halfbreeds who led Indian style lives and supplied the pemmican on which the *voyageurs* depended in their far-ranging journeys.

Selkirk planted his colony of farmers on Indian and Metis lands squarely across the route of the North West Company's fur trade. From his point of view this was perfectly legitimate because the whole of the northwest belonged to his company under the charter granted by King

Papineau's rebels being dispersed by government troops at St Eustache, in the Province of Quebec, 1837.

Successful settlement of the Red River country depended in part on friendly negotiations with the local Indians.

Charles II almost two centuries earlier.

North Westers, Metis, and a party of Indians laid siege to the Red River Settlement, and, the following year, killed Selkirk's representative and 21 of his colonists. He replied by invading the west in person with a brigade of Swiss mercenaries, capturing and ransacking the posts of the North West Company. In the end the company was forced to capitulate, to allow itself, its posts and its assets to be absorbed by The Bay in a nominal merger that was in fact mere face saving.

The Red River settlers remained, helping to cause the wars, 'rebellions' and fratricidal turmoil that made the Canadian west a no-man's land for the next 60 years. A group of chiefs from the Cree, Assiniboine and Salteaux tribes was tricked into signing the first treaty with the Hudson's Bay Company in 1817. In a long series of such swindles the Indians of the Canadian west were stripped of everything they owned—their land, their buffalo, their way of life.

Meanwhile, rebellion flared in both Upper and Lower Canada. As early as 1819 the reformer Robert Gourlay was banished from Upper Canada for seditious treason. By the 1830s bands of rebels were organizing in Ontario under William Lyon Mackenzie, and in Quebec under Louis-Joseph Papineau.

Mackenzie was the owner of a reform newspaper which lasted for two years before a band of Tories raided his offices and threw his press into Toronto's Don River. He sued, collected damages, and published more vigorously than ever, attacking the rule of the family compact, a band of *nouveau riche* English who had established themselves as the local aristocracy.

In 1834 the Reform Party was elected in Upper Canada, and the legislature of Lower Canada passed the Ninety-two Resolutions—a statement of the grievances suffered by the Quebecois under the colonial government. Nothing happened. The grievances remained, aggravated by a severe economic depression. Then, after two years in office, the Reform Party was defeated, and rebels in both colonies began to take up arms.

The rebellion in Upper Canada, led by Mackenzie, was little more than an armed demonstration. It never seriously tried to seize the government, was easily suppressed, and Mackenzie fled into exile in the United States with a price of a thousand British pounds on his head. His deputy Samuel Lount was hanged.

Papineau was a political leader who had spent 20 years in the legislature fighting in vain for the rights of his people. When this failed he joined the *Patriotes* in armed rebellion. It was crushed by regular troops as decisively as the rebellion in Upper Canada, but with much greater difficulty. The army's camp followers and volunteers then went on a campaign of looting and burning that turned most of the *Quebecois* into embittered haters of the British. Papineau fled to the United States, but more widespread and better-organized rebellion followed in Lower Canada.

This second revolt was suppressed with great brutality. The army marched through Quebec burning farms and villages as they went, driving the *habitants* into the woods, seizing men as prisoners, abandoning homeless women and children to starve or freeze to death. In Quebec 1200 rebels were thrown into jail, 98 were tried for treason, 12 were hanged and 58 were transported to the living hell of the Australian penal colonies.

In Upper Canada 885 were jailed, 20 were hanged, and 92 were transported. But in the midst of it all the British discovered that they were creating national martyrs and heroes, both in Upper and Lower Canada, and had the sense to stop the executions.

Following the rebellion of 1834 Queen Victoria appointed the Earl of Durham as Governor General with instructions to find the cause and the cure. Within a year he presented a massive report on which a new constitution was based. It provided for a single legislature with equal numbers of members from Quebec and Ontario. The United Colony was given control of its revenues and expenditures, taxation could be levied only by the legislature, and the governor was instructed not to oppose the Assembly unless the honor of the crown or the interests of the Empire were deeply concerned. It satisfied neither the reformers nor the Family Compact, but effected a compromise that everyone managed to live with until confederation, a quarter of a century later.

Equally important was the settlement in 1854 of the seigneurial question in Quebec. These land rights, dating back to the reign of Louis XIV and even earlier, made tenants of most Quebec farmers. The seigneuries were purchased by the Canadian government, and Quebec citizens given freehold title to their land.

This was also the era of the great influx of immigrants from Europe. Scots, Irish and English, with a sprinkling of Germans and Swiss, they flooded into Canada by the tens of thousands every year. Some of them settled in Quebec, but most went on to Ontario to open up vast tracts of farmland northward from Lake Erie and Lake Ontario. The flood crested in 1832, when 66,000 immigrants settled in Upper Canada.

The opening of the west also continued apace. The Hudson's Bay Company founded Edmonton House in 1823, and Fort Vancouver in 1825. Settlers began moving westward from the Red River to the Assiniboine and the Saskatchewan. There was still no government anywhere in the west, however, none except the local councils of the Metis, and the distant lordship of the Hudson's Bay Company exercised through a few armed forts and posts.

Despite the lack of government, the Canadian west was never a lawless frontier. The Indians were self-governing and well organized. The Metis also led orderly lives under the leadership of master hunters who organized the great annual buffalo drives. Here and there a murder took place, here and there an armed clash between rival factions, but there was almost none of the free-wheeling gun-slinging that entered so deeply into the American consciousness, and helped make the 'American Dream' so fundamentally different from the Canadian.

Canada had discovered a sense of nationhood in the War of 1812, when British and French fought side by side, Nova Scotia privateers played hell with American shipping, and the Newfoundland regiment known as 'Skinner's Fencibles' came to the defense of Canada, as a Newfoundland regiment had done during the American War of Independence. This sense did not begin to take political shape until the 1860s. Meanwhile, settlers had flocked to British Columbia, a legislature was sitting on Vancouver Island, fishing and lumbering industries were flourishing, and Victoria was considering incorporation. It became British Columbia's first city in 1862, in the midst of the

Louis Joseph Papineau (1786–1871), French-Canadian political insurgent, whose followers in Quebec openly rebelled in 1837. He received amnesty in 1844.

great Cariboo gold rush that brought a new wave of immigrants to Canada's west coast.

The population was now over 3 million, six times larger than it had been in 1800, but it was dispersed in such widely separated areas that none but a few dreamers even envisioned a nation 'from sea to sea'. Ontario and Quebec (then called Canada East and Canada West) were united with equal representation in a single parliament. All the other colonies had ties directly with England. Nova Scotia was experiencing an industrial boom that made any alliance outside her immediate area look unattractive. Newfoundland and British Columbia were both so physically remote from the rest of Canada that the idea of union seemed absurd, and both had close commercial ties with the United States.

The few dreamers included John A Macdonald, the young Kingston lawyer who had become the most powerful Ontario politician, and George-Etienne Cartier, the undisputed leader of Quebec, who not only believed in confederation, but convinced most of his countrymen, as well.

It began as a meeting in Charlottetown, Prince Edward Island, to discuss a merger of the Atlantic colonies. Delegates from the two Canadas crashed the party (September 1864) and convinced the Martimers that what they ought to be talking about was not Atlantic Union but a union of British North America. The bait was a railway linking Halifax and St John with Montreal, to be financed mainly by the two Canadas. Since building railways had nearly bankrupted the governments of Nova Scotia and New Brunswick, it looked tempting. There was much less in it for Newfoundland or Prince Edward Island, but they, too, agreed to attend, and Newfoundland sent the strongest pro-confederate politicians in the province.

The only eastern province really convinced was New Brunswick. Prince Edward Island and Newfoundland quickly elected anti-confederate governments, and Nova Scotia did the same. But before the Nova Scotia elections, the pro-confederate premier had managed to get a motion carried in its favour. So Nova Scotia came into the union in spite of itself. A petition to the Queen from the Nova Scotia Legislature to annul an act so flagrantly against the wishes of the people had no effect. The British North American Act, passed by Britain, united the four provinces of Ontario, Quebec, New Brunswick and Nova Scotia. The Nova Scotians did, however, create enough fuss to get the terms of union renegotiated, thus offsetting some of the economic loss that confederation threatened to their trade, their manufacturing, and their great shipbuilding industries.

Confederation of the four provinces took effect on July 1, 1867. That same year the British Columbia legislature approved an Act to enable its government to negotiate Confederation, though the distant colony did not actually enter the union until 1871. Prince Edward Island continued to stand aloof until 1873, and Newfoundland for almost a century.

29

The New Dominion

The first Dominion Day, 1 July 1867, was celebrated with rejoicing in Ontario, crowds in the streets, flags flying. It was generally ignored in Quebec. In Halifax the flags were at half mast and black crepe was hung over the doors.

One of the first major acts of the new Dominion of Canada was to buy Rupert's Land from the Hudson's Bay Company. This gave Canada not only the Arctic, including what are now northern Ontario and Quebec, but the whole of what later became the western provinces, right to the border of British Columbia. In ten years, the wild dream had become a reality, and the nation stretched from sea to sea.

True, serious problems remained. Most serious of all was the fact that the Hudson's Bay Company had no moral right to own or sell lands that belonged to the Indians and the Metis. Throughout this whole territory, larger than the continental United States, there were only about 2000 English-speaking settlers and Hudson's Bay employees, but there were many thousands of Indians (their numbers not even estimated) and 6000 French-speaking Metis, with various degrees of Indian ancestry.

There was no thought, in Ottawa, the new capital, of preserving land rights or native lifestyles. The idea was to occupy the west with European settlers as quickly as possible to keep it from being colonized by Americans. These had already arrived; hordes of armed ex-soldiers who had fought in the War Between the States, now free to seek their fortunes, swarmed into the Great Plains and over the Canadian border, trading rot-gut whiskey to the Indians and building forts that bristled with small cannon.

They not only thoroughly corrupted and impoverished the Indians who agreed to trade with them, but they also introduced a raging epidemic of syphilis and smallpox that had killed at least 10,000 people by 1870.

The repeating rifles that they traded along with whiskey made the decimation of the buf-

falo herds, already depleted, into an imminent disaster. The people of the Plains, Indian and Metis, depended entirely on buffalo for their livelihood, their food, their clothing, their tents, even for horse harness and bone implements. By 1869 the governments in Washington and Ottawa both knew that the buffalo were being exterminated. They not only made no effort to save the greatest meat resource on the continent, but approved the slaughter. The buffalo, like the forests, were a nuisance standing in the

New immigrants on a Montreal quay in the mid-19th century. Most of them then pushed on to English-speaking Canada.

way of settlement—best to turn their hides into cash as quickly as possible.

After Sir John A Macdonald, Canada's first Prime Minister, completed the purchase of Rupert's Land, he sent out William McDougall as governor. McDougall approached Fort Gary (now Winnipeg) through Minnesota, but was met at the border by a band of armed Metis who refused to allow him to enter. They had set up their own provisional government under their leader Louis Riel, and wished to negotiate with the government of Canada for a Metis bill of rights.

The Metis professed loyalty to the Queen, but wished to enter the Canadian Union on their own terms. The Government of Canada ignored them, but nevertheless passed the Manitoba Act, making that territory a separate province, recognizing the Metis land claims, and guaranteeing rights of language and religion. Riel, however, was treated as an outlaw; the only leader who could have stood up for his province and made its entry into Confederation a just one, had to flee for his life to the United States.

It was a period of great technological advance. Ontario's first steam locomotive arrived in October 1852, three years later the line from Niagara Falls to Detroit was operating, and a line to Lake Huron's Georgian Bay was being built.

All important cities were linked by telegraph line, and then, dramatically, to Europe: the steamship Great Eastern landed the first successful trans-ocean cable at Heart's Content, Newfoundland on 27 July 1866. The next year a second cable was added.

Street railways opened in the major cities. Steamships were built and launched as far west

The extermination of the buffalo was a direct cause of the rebellions of the Metis. INSET: Louis Riel.
OPPOSITE: Left to right—Sir John A Macdonald, William Lyon Mackenzie, Alexander Mackenzie.

as the Red River in Manitoba. Toronto began manufacturing clocks, pianos, and finally locomotives. Prospectors struck oil in southwestern Ontario, and within two years there were 27 refineries.

Montreal and Quebec were still the largest cities in Canada, with 100,000 and 52,000 people respectively. Toronto ranked next, with 49,000, and the three major ports—St John's, Halifax and St John—had about 30,000 each.

In the far west, it was gold. After the California fields had been exhausted, the Cariboo, in British Columbia, became the richest in the world, producing tens of millions of dollars in nuggets and dust, but the wealth was temporary, producing little permanent development, but huge profits for merchants, bankers and distillers, all of whom had their headquarters elsewhere. The overlanders who had hoped for fortunes in gold wound up working in the logging and fishing industries, or drifted south as land-settlers and cowpunchers in the opening American west.

The greatest achievement of the gold rush was the Cariboo Trail, 400 miles of all-weather mountain highway built at a cost of a million dollars, linking the interior goldfield with the coast. An engineering triumph, it was perhaps the finest road on the continent, and promoted British Columbia from a mere collection of coastal settlements to a province with a rich

and varied hinterland.

Between 1871 and 1877 the Government of Canada signed seven treaties with the various bands of the Plains Indians. Collectively, they gave the Crown title to hundreds of thousands of square miles of land in exchange for a few tools like hoes and axes, a few animals such as horses and pigs, an absolutely insignificant amount of money, and police protection against the whiskey traders.

The land could then be parcelled out among white settlers, and the Indians herded on reservations where they, too, were supposed to farm without any traditions or skills for farming, whether the land could grow crops or not.

The only part of the deal of any benefit to the Indians was police protection. The Northwest Mounted Police, founded in 1873, immediately established a reputation for fearlessness, justice and impartiality. They promptly stopped the whiskey trade. They enforced the law with a show of fearless authority. They gained such respect that they could ride into a hostile village and stop a local feud without having to resort to violence.

South of the border there was no such rule of law. The Army ranged far and wide, slaughtering the buffalo as a means of starving the warlike Sioux into submission. 'Sportsmen' helped by seeing how many animals they could slaughter from a moving train. Grass fires, deliberately set to prevent migration, trapped vast herds of the animals. By the end of the decade the Canadian government had recognized some obligation toward the buffalo herds, and in 1877 outlawed the practice of driving the animals over cliffs. The measure was meaningless. By then the buffalo were virtually extinct.

It was an era of great political happenings. Macdonald's and Cartier's Tories entered Confederation with a solid hold on the Federal Government, but by 1873, they came crashing down in the great Pacific Scandal, when it was proved beyond argument that they had taken at least $350,000 in party funds from the contractors for the Canadian Pacific Railway. The Grits, headed by Alexander Mackenzie, formed a government and were confirmed in power by the general election of 1874. Nobody expected Macdonald to recover from this total disgrace. But economic depression saved him. By 1878 Canada was experiencing such hard times that Macdonald was able to regain power on a platform of protective tariffs, and hold it till his death in 1891.

Confederation was almost, but not quite, completed in the 1870s. First Manitoba was drafted into the union by Act of Parliament (1870) then British Columbia, tempted by the promise of the Canadian Pacific, agreed to implement its enabling act and enter the union (1871) and finally Prince Edward Island, almost bankrupted by building a railway, agreed to join for a straight cash settlement and federal assumption of the railway liability (1873).

That same year, Louis Riel, the 'rebel,' was

elected to Parliament from Manitoba (he was never allowed to take his seat) and Winnipeg was incorporated as a city. The Niagara was bridged at Fort Erie—the fear of American aggression had been laid to rest.

Economic development rushed forward at headlong speed. In 1876 the Intercolonial Railway was completed, linking Ontario and Quebec to the Maritimes. The Massey manufacturing firm, starting as a small foundry in the town of Cobourg, quickly became a world leader in the manufacture of farm machinery, and absorbed many other firms as it expanded. Alexander Graham Bell introduced the telephone in 1876, and two years later the first exchange was opened at Hamilton. Bell, a Scot, lived at Brantford, Ontario, worked at a Boston school for the deaf, but did most of his later work, on subjects including aircraft and hydrofoils, at his estate near Baddeck, Nova Scotia. Cyrille Duquet, a Quebec inventor, patented an improved telephone in 1878.

The population of Canada, including Newfoundland, was now over four million, 80 percent of it still rural, and still engaged overwhelmingly in primary production—farming, fishing, logging and mining. Much of the produce, including timber, was exported as raw material to be manufactured in Europe and the United States.

Light industry had developed early. Quebec was manufacturing furniture from local and imported woods even in the 17th century, and continued to be a centre of such artisan industry throughout the 18th and 19th centuries. Foundries, brick works, breweries, all flourished in the towns and cities of French Canada, and extended to other provinces as they became populated. Clothing manufacture, boots and shoes, manufacture of lines and ropes existed in Quebec, and formed the basis of industries that had reached the level of national importance before the end of the 19th century. The Atlantic Provinces manufactured ships' hardware, hawsers, anchors, nails, bolts, stoves, paints and varnishes.

Industry spread across the nation, as the population spread, but the day of heavy industry, based on smelting and rolling mills, cutting dies and patterns for machinery, was just begin-

Big Bear, a Cree chief, another ally of Riel, who was arrested and jailed for two years, dying of a broken spirit.

ning—and beginning mainly in Ontario. This province, founded by fur traders and farmers, was soon to become not just the industrial centre of the nation, but its *imperial* centre as well, a centre that would dictate the economic condition of the other provinces, and eventually lead to stresses threatening the very existence of Canada.

After buying Rupert's Land, the new nation's next great project was to build a transcontinental railway—the Canadian Pacific. It seemed highly risky—and indeed was: it not only tempted the great Conservative Party to a near-fatal flirtation with large-scale graft, but nearly bankrupted the government as well. It also set the match to the smouldering fuse of the northwest rebellion.

The so-called rebellion that created the Province of Manitoba was no true rebellion at all, since there was no government in the region except the provisional one organized by Louis Riel. The rebellion that led to the creation of Saskatchewan and Alberta was a true revolt against the established rule of the governor and the Northwest Mounted Police who enforced his decrees. It began with an armed attack on a

Chief Poundmaker in a photograph taken about 1886. This Indian leader was an ally of Riel in the rebellion.

police column, and ended with a full-scale battle in which regular soldiers supported by artillery gradually reduced the rebel capital of Batouche to submission.

The rebellion was incited by the railway, by the surveying of lands already occupied for sale in lots to settlers, by the government's failure to provide relief for Indians reduced to starvation by the destruction of the buffalo, and by the obdurate refusal of leaders in Ottawa to discuss those grievances with representatives of the Indians, the Metis and the settlers.

As the buffalo were exterminated, famine spread among all the Indians of the plains, and hardship among the Metis. The latter took up farming with some success, but the Indians who tried it failed miserably. Many of the white settlers, like the Metis, had entered the country before land titles could be acquired, and suffered the same danger of dispossession. They joined the agitation, but deserted the cause when protest turned to armed rebellion.

It was a time for swift and decisive action, for setting up a new province, for granting local self-government, and for recognizing the land claims of both Metis and Indians. Instead of do-ing this, the government in Ottawa did nothing. By the spring of 1884 the people of the west were so desperate that they held a meeting and decided to invite Louis Riel back from his exile in Montana. He had forced the Federal Government to create the Province of Manitoba, almost without bloodshed. Perhaps, now, he could do the same for the people further west.

Riel accepted, met the Metis at Batouche, and dispatched a petition to Ottawa calling for provincial status, guaranteed land rights and a railway link to Hudson's Bay. Instead of replying to these demands, the government began to call up troops, and the Metis began to form themselves into a militia.

Riel set up his second provisional government at Batouche in March 1885. The Federal Government rushed 5000 troops westward over the partially completed railway. Using field guns and some of the first machine guns ever used in warfare, the troops soon captured the Metis forts, took Riel prisoner, and received the submission of the Indian chiefs Poundmaker and Big Bear.

Eight of the Indians were hanged, and Riel, too, was hanged for treason, despite widespread petitions for his pardon. Fifty thousand people in Montreal demonstrated against the hanging, which had been demanded by Ontario's Orange Society (an anti-Catholic league founded in Northern Ireland.) It was regarded not only in Quebec, but also in Britain and the United States, as an act of irrational vengeance.

Twenty years later, the Northwest, which in a moment of desperation had called Riel out of exile, became the provinces of Saskatchewan and Alberta. Canada now consisted of nine provinces stretching from the Atlantic to the Pacific, and a vast northern territory stretching from Baffin Island to the border of Alaska, administered (in name only) by the Federal Government. In fact no government official set foot in any part of this territory for years at a stretch. It was owned and occupied by the northern Indians and the Inuit, and merely 'claimed' by Canada. It would not actually be occupied, even by visiting officials, until the time of the Second World War.

The only part of the north effectively occupied by Canada was the Yukon, and this only

because a wandering prospector discovered gold in the streambed of the Klondike River in 1898. Thousands of fortune seekers, not only from all parts of Canada, but also from all parts of North America and Europe, headed north from the Alaska panhandle over rock and snow and ice into the Canadian Arctic, to effect the first real opening of the north.

Meanwhile the railway had been completed not only to the Pacific, but also into the mining regions of British Columbia, with spur lines to the wheat farming areas of the west, and a veritable network of lines throughout the east. Before the railway boom was over, there were to be three lines across Canada, serving to open the country from west to east, and from south to north—at least so far north as Prince Albert, Edmonton, and Prince Rupert.

In this period, too, the railway was completed across Newfoundland from St John's to Port aux Basques, touching the northern bays en route, and opening up the country to the forest industries, mainly pulp and paper, which were soon to replace fish as Newfoundland's major exports.

Mining for metals other than gold also became important, especially on the Canadian Shield, an area of ancient rocks stretching from Newfoundland through northern Quebec and Ontario into the Northwest Territories. Copper, silver, lead, zinc and iron were mined on various parts of the Shield from Newfoundland to Northern Ontario. Later nickel became important in Ontario and asbestos in Quebec. Vast coal fields were discovered in Nova Scotia, and, wedded to Newfoundland's iron, produced a great steel industry on Cape Breton Island.

The Prime Minister of Canada, at the turn of the century, was Sir Wilfrid Laurier, the first Quebec politician to head a Federal Government, and the first Liberal Party leader to hold office for more than one term. He held power for 15 years from 1896 until 1911, made the Liberals the supreme force in Canadian politics, and founded the tradition that French Canadians and English Canadians succeed each other as Liberal party leaders, a tradition that has continued for almost a century, and that has contributed immensely to the success of the Liberals from Laurier's time to the present. Laurier coined the phrase: 'The twentieth century belongs to Canada.' The industrial, farming and mining booms that happened in his time made it look like a safe prophecy.

As the new century dawned, Canada looked like the land of the future. A great wheat boom filled the west with immigrants. Every year thousands of square miles of former buffalo pasture were ploughed and seeded. Prices

Cabot Tower on Signal Hill, St John's, Newfoundland, where, in 1901, Guglielmo Marconi sent his first wireless signal to Cornwall, England, and received an answer.

soared, and men who had never seen a grain elevator made fortunes in wheat futures. Even the farmers, once they had built their first sod homesteads and broken their first hundred acres, made a comfortable living.

Exciting things happened everywhere. At Baddeck in Nova Scotia Canadians were among the pioneers of the air, contemporaries of the Wrights, and first in the British Commonwealth to fly heavier-than-air machines. On Signal Hill in Newfoundland Marconi sent up a kite with a wire aerial, and received the first trans-ocean wireless message. R A Fessenden of Quebec was first in the world to transmit the human voice by wireless. Vancouver was linked by cable with Australia. A new gold field was discovered in northern Ontario. The world's first successful hydrofoil ship was built and tested in Nova Scotia. All this, and much more, in the century's first ten years.

The map of Canada was completed by explorers. Roald Amundsen navigated the Northwest Passage, the first success after four centuries of trials and the loss of hundreds of lives. Frederick Cook and Robert Peary explored Canada's arctic islands as jumping-off places for sledge journeys to the north pole. By 1909 both were claiming success. Otto Sverdrup mapped the last major land masses in the north, and Vilhjalmur Stefansson filled in the last small islands that Sverdrup had missed. Robert Bartlett, the Newfoundland captain who had taken Peary to within 150 miles of the pole, performed the nearly superhuman feat of rescuing the remnants of Stefansson's expedition, stranded on drift ice in mid winter far to the north of Siberia.

The flood of immigrants crested in 1913, when more than 400,000 settlers arrived, most of them looking for land. More gold was discovered in Ontario, oil and gas in Alberta.

The population passed eight million.

Public health was deplorable, especially in the cities, where public sanitation and clean water were still things of the future. Tuberculosis was endemic. There were annual epidemics of infectious diseases, especially among children. In working-class Montreal, Canada's biggest city with a population of over half a million, the infant mortality rate stood at 26.8 percent of live births.

But life was happy—at least for those a little above the working class. Times were good. Money was plentiful. Dance halls flourished. Live theatre, movie houses, music halls, concerts, operas, all contended for their share of the wealth.

And then came the crash. By 1914 the boom had turned to a bust. Breadlines and soup kitchens opened for the destitute. The First World War came along just in time to gather the legions of the unemployed into the legions of the damned.

Canada entered the First World War as a colony and emerged from it as a nation. Though a national spirit had been born in the War of 1812, and a national economy had begun to emerge with the building of the Canadian Pacific, it was not until the Canadian army went to Europe and insisted on fighting as a unit under its own leaders, that the chains of dependency tying it to Great Britain began to be cut.

The war was a quarrel between European imperial powers whose interests were not those of Canada. Nevertheless, when they began fighting in August 1914, Canada found herself *automatically at war*. In foreign affairs she was still legally a British dependency.

The first move toward independence came when the Defence Minister, Colonel Sam Hughes, refused to allow the Canadian Expeditionary Force to be broken up and scattered among British formations, as the British Minister of War, Lord Kitchener, had planned to do. They fought as Canadian divisions at first separately, then united under a single command, and finally, in 1918, as an army of shock troops, leaders of the assault that broke through the German defences and ended the war.

Canada and Newfoundland (still a separate colony) sent more than half a million men to fight in the First World War. They suffered a quarter of a million casualties.

It was a four-year hell of mud, filth, rotting corpses, rats, lice, and slow or sudden death. Most of the war was a stalemate with opposing armies dug in only a few score yards apart. The only tactic the generals knew was to send men on foot with bayonets in suicidal charges against trenches defended by machine guns. Millions were mowed down.

In April 1915 the Canadians withstood the first poison gas attack at Ypres, and two weeks of savage fighting in a futile attempt by the Germans to break the allied line. The 1st Canadian Division lost more than a fifth of its men, and some units—Saskatchewan's Fifth Regiment, British Columbia's Gordon Highlanders—were virtually wiped out.

In 1916, at the Battle of the Somme, losses

were even worse. On 1 July the Royal New-foundland Regiment was slaughtered at Beaumont Hamel, and Canada's national holiday has been observed in Newfoundland as a day of mourning ever since. After over a million casualties at the Somme, the fighting ground to a halt a few hundred yards from where it had begun.

The first major Canadian victory came when the army captured Vimy Ridge in April 1917, at a terrible cost in killed and wounded. It was the first of a series of 'shock troop' battles for the Canadians that culminated the following year when they broke through the Germans' Hindenburg Line and crossed the border into Belgium in one of the crucial battles leading to the German surrender.

Lieut Col W A 'Billy' Bishop of Owen Sound, Ontario, was the highest-scoring fighter pilot in the British Services during World War I, being credited with shooting down 72 planes.

Men of the Canadian Corps going over the top during the Battle
of the Somme, September 1916.
BELOW: Many Canadian Indians joined the armed forces during
World War I—a photograph of 1916.
LEFT: Billy Bishop

The Empress Theatre on 8th Avenue in Calgary in the 1920s.
Prices: Children 6¢, Adults 32½¢.
RIGHT: In the 1920s the ham radio was all the rage in Canada.

Besides those who served in the armies (allied as well as Canadian), thousands of men, especially from Newfoundland and Nova Scotia, served in the Royal Navy. Best remembered, though, are the young 'aces' who flew with the Royal Flying Corps. For some reason hard to explain, Canadians distinguished themselves in the air, flying the kite-like contraptions armed with machine guns that were the most advanced airplanes of their time. A Canadian, Roy Brown, shot down the most famous German ace, Manfred von Richthofen. Another, Billy Bishop, accounted for 72 enemy aircraft. Two of the war's five top aces were Canadians, and there were eight others with 30 or more aerial victories to their credit.

When peace returned, the country went mad

over airplanes. New records for speed, distance or endurance were made almost monthly. Oxygen masks made high altitudes attainable, and men soared to heights believed to be impossible only a decade before.

The first really major prize was to fly the Atlantic. Many tried and failed. Some vanished. Some were fished out of the sea. One 'flying boat,' forced down in mid-ocean, managed to reach the Azores by taxiing along the surface. The first to succeed was a team of Britishers, Alcock and Brown, who took off from Newfoundland on 14 June 1919, and landed in Ireland 17 hours later. This so stirred the tiny dominion that Newfoundland rushed to complete its first 'aerodrome' at Harbour Grace, which then became the takeoff point for many trans-ocean flights. Navigation was accurate only in clear weather. One German team, unable to get above the overcast, missed Harbour Grace by four hundred miles, and crash landed on the coast of Labrador.

By the end of the 1920s the single-engined plane had become the normal means of transport to the northern bush and the barren Arctic. Air mail deliveries, passenger flights, stunt and thrill flying were common. For five dollars anyone could buy a 15 minute flight over his home town, and if his nerves could stand it the pilot would do a side slip and an inside loop to make the experience unforgettable. Light biplanes such as the Gipsy Moth were favorites for this kind of flying, but there were other planes just taking to the air that could lift two dozen passengers or two tons of freight—multi-engined metal monsters replacing the wood-canvas-and-wire birds of aviation's first two decades.

It was the age of the ice cream parlour, the flapper and the nightclub, institutions that became trademarks of the Twenties. But it was also one of great social unrest.

Women had been agitating for the right to vote, believing they could change society if given the chance. Women in the armed forces and immediate relatives of men serving overseas, voted during the war. By war's end this had been extended, in most parts of Canada, to all women 21 years or older. Agnes Macphail was elected and entered Parliament in 1921.

Organized labour began for the first time to be a major social force. Canada was shocked into the new age by the Winnipeg general strike—a strike that began with metal workers demanding higher wages and quickly spread through sympathy strikes until more than 30,000 workers were idle, and all public services, as well as private business, came to a halt. Even the police joined the strikers in the spring of 1919, and effective government passed from city hall to the strike headquarters.

The strike was broken by violence. Squads of armed federal police were brought in as strike-breakers. They clubbed and shot demonstrators in the streets, killed two men, sent 30 to hospital and 91 to jail. Eight of the strike leaders were sentenced to prison—terms ranging from six months to two years. Others were acquitted, including J S Woodsworth, who was to found the democratic socialist party known as the Co-operative Commonwealth Federation. After Mackenzie King, the Liberal Party leader, Woodsworth was the most influential political leader in Canada in the years between the two world wars.

Farmers, too, began to organize, and gained quick political success. Between 1919 and 1922 the United Farmers of Ontario, Alberta and Manitoba captured the governments of those three provinces. Even in Newfoundland the Fishermen's Protective Union was able to force the Liberals into a coalition. To fight federal elections the farmers formed the Progressive Party, sent 65 members to Parliament, and ended the 'two party system' in Canada once and for all. Since the 1920s there has always been at least one party of the Left represented in Parliament, frequently strong enough to force minority governments to introduce progressive legislation. The Progressives did not last long. They were replaced by the CCF, and then by the New Democrats. But the 'third force' remained strong enough, under whatever name, to introduce old—age pensions, workmen's compensation and unemployment insurance, family allowances, socialized medicine, transfer payments for health and education, and numerous other measures that tended to reduce the harsh social inequalities of the past and the exploitation of the working class.

The boom of the early 1900s was repeated in the 1920s, this time with the added frill of mass stock speculation. On 25 October 1929 the New York stock market collapsed, followed by the stock markets in other cities, including Montreal and Toronto and Winnipeg. Within a few months thousands of corporations were bankrupt, millions were unemployed, and consumer purchasing power fell so low that most manufacturing plants had to go on part time, lay off staff, or close altogether.

Revenues of provincial governments fell so low that some of them could not pay interest on their bonds. The same thing happened in Newfoundland, where the Dominion Government, by 1932, was unable to finance the debt the tiny nation had accumulated to finance its part in the First World War and the modest public works that had followed. The Government of Great Britain agreed to guarantee the debt (in fact they never had to put up any actual money) on condition that Newfoundland abandon the status of a self-governing dominion and accept government by an appointed commission. This, as it turned out, was the first step toward Newfoundland's joining the Canadian union.

The Depression, as it came to be called, lasted through most of the 1930s, but reached its absolute depth in 1932 and 1933. Canada was hit very hard, especially on the Prairies, where most people relied exclusively on wheat farming, and wheat became so unsaleable that people burned it for fuel. But over much of the west a disastrous drought added to the misery. Land that should never have been ploughed in the first place now turned to dust and drifted over fences and houses, turning a once-green landscape into a desert. People escaped to the cities, to the west coast, to the east, by whatever means they could find, travelling in carts, broken down cars, on freight trains. And in the cities they formed endless breadlines, crowded into charity shelters for the homeless, slept in church basements, or, if they were young men, went off to government labour camps where they were paid twenty cents a day.

The unemployed in the cities were little better off than the farmers who stayed in the dust bowl of the west. Mixed subsistence farming and fishing made life a little easier in some parts of Canada—rural Nova Social and Newfoundland, the St Lawrence Valley—where people could gather their own fuel, grow or catch most of their own food, but even in these places there were a few instances of outright starvation, and many deaths from the diseases of deficiency and malnutrition.

There were riots in the streets. In April 1932 a mob attacked the Newfoundland parliament buildings and tried to lynch the Prime Minister. On Dominion Day 1935, a peaceful demonstration of the unemployed in Regina was attacked by the Royal Canadian Mounted Police. The demonstrators responded by building barricades in the streets and wrecking the town in a looting spree. One policeman was killed, scores of rioters were wounded and the unemployed marchers, sleeping on straw on the Exhibition Grounds, awoke next day to find the gates guarded by police with mounted machine guns. The unemployed were sent back to the labour camps.

In the midst of the hunger, despair and social misery of the Thirties there were signs of progress, both social and technological. Norman Bethune, the Canadian doctor who was later to become one of the heroes of the Chinese struggle against Japan, opened a free medical clinic for the destitute in Montreal. When the Fascist army under General Franco invaded Spain from North Africa in 1936 Bethune went to Spain and organized the world's first mobile blood clinics.

Canada continued to be a leader in air transport, especially in using planes as freighters. In 1935 Edmonton airport handled 26 million pounds of freight, more than the combined air freight of the United States, Britain, France and Germany.

Trans Canada Air Lines (later to be Air Canada) began commercial flights in 1937, and by 1939 were carrying passengers on scheduled flights between Montreal and Vancouver. A year later they had extended their service to the Maritimes and Newfoundland.

OPPOSITE TOP: The Regina Riot of 1 July 1935.
INSET: Prime Minister Richard Bedford Bennett (1870–1947).
BOTTOM: A demonstration by the unemployed, 1933.

King George VI and Queen Elizabeth opening the Parliament in Ottawa, 1939.
OPPOSITE: A Canadian soldier departing for service in Europe, 1940, saying goodbye to his son.
INSET: Canadian soldiers heading for the Western Front, 1940.

Radio replaced newspapers as the major means of communication. 'Wind chargers' appeared everywhere on farms, generating electricity for those beyond the range of power lines. Radios and telephones also operated from dry cell battery packs. The Canadian Broadcasting Corporation was created by Act of Parliament in 1936 to give Canadians an alternative to the popular American networks.

At the beginning of the Depression, the Liberals were blamed for inaction, and the Tories under R B Bennett formed the first majority government in Canada in a decade. Five years later the Tories were blamed for making the Depression even worse, and the Liberals, under Mackenzie King, were returned by a landslide.

The change of government made no real difference. The country was slowly pulling out of the Depression, and world markets were slowly recovering, so that Canada could once more sell its products abroad, when the Second World War started, and governments that could not feed their people suddenly found it difficult to find enough hands to man the ships, the production lines, grow the wheat, drive the machines, and handle the freight in ports where dock workers went on 24-hour shifts in an effort to cope with the sudden flow of goods.

At the end of the First World War Canada had insisted on separate status at the Peace Conference and in the League of Nations. No longer was Canada automatically at war because Britain had declared war on Hitler's Germany. But there was no question that the sentiment of the country was overwhelmingly of the opinion that Hitler had to be stopped, and that it was the duty of every democratic country in the world to take part in what amounted to a crusade against Nazism.

Mackenzie King, always cautious, waited a week before declaring war. During that week Newfoundland had already seized German ships and interned their crews, and the Canadian army, with a peacetime strength of about 10,000, had bought every bit of American equipment it could lay hands on, rushing tanks and transports and self-propelled guns across the border before Canada became a belligerent, and ineligible to buy arms.

There was an instant rush to join the Canadian forces. Thousands of men who had never had jobs of any kind jumped at the chance to carry a gun for regular pay, decent clothes, good food, and the booze and women that were part of every soldier's birthright. The navy was especially popular among those who remembered that it had suffered only light casualties in the former war, while field soldiers were butchered by the millions. The air force was popular for another reason—its pure glamour. This time there would be a separate Canadian navy, Canadian army, and Canadian air force. Only Newfoundlanders served as regular elements of the British army—two regiments of field artillery—though many still preferred the navy, and many of them died in the desperate convoy battles that made this war at sea so different from the last.

Except for the swift conquest of Poland, little happened during the first six months of the war. Then, in a space of ten weeks in the spring of 1940, Germany overran Denmark, Norway, Holland, Belgium and France. Britain was isolated, threatened with invasion, and in danger of being starved into submission.

The Battle of Britain was fought in the air that summer, and won by the Royal Air Force

ABOVE: French-Canadian volunteers leaving to embark for
Hong Kong, 17 November 1941.
RIGHT: Canadians arriving in Hong Kong, 13 November 1941.
BELOW: Canadian dead in Hong Kong.

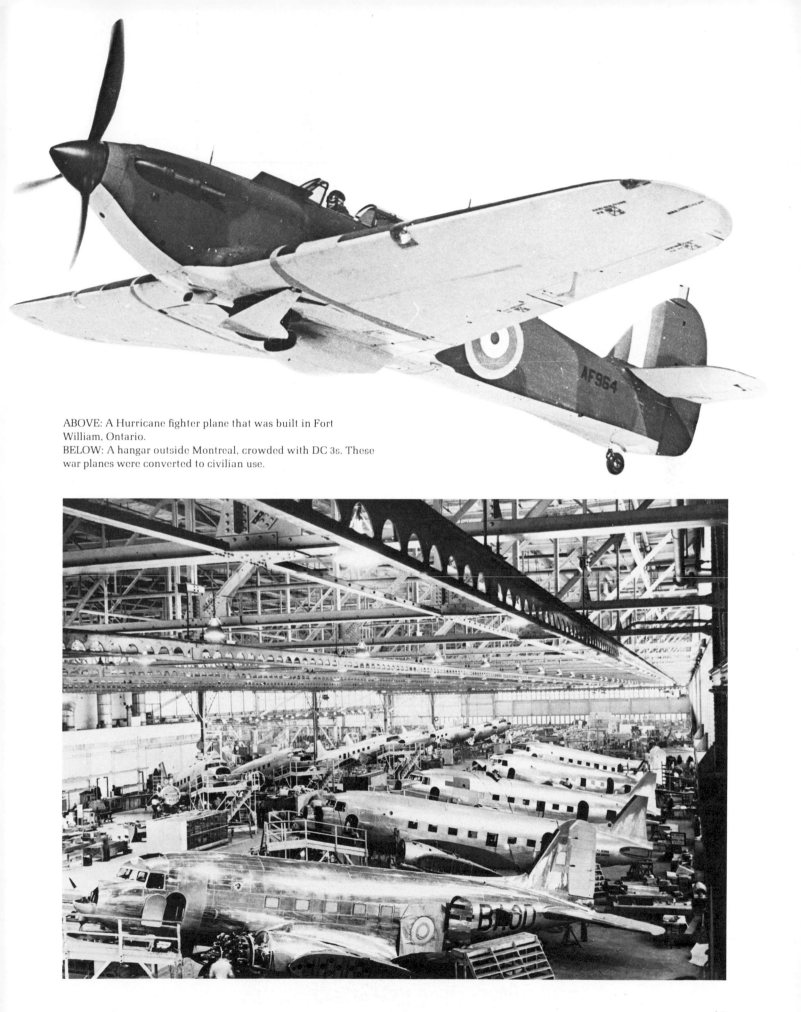

ABOVE: A Hurricane fighter plane that was built in Fort William, Ontario.
BELOW: A hangar outside Montreal, crowded with DC 3s. These war planes were converted to civilian use.

against great odds. The Battle of the Atlantic, which could have defeated her just as decisively, dragged on for years, and it was here that Canada's role was vital.

The first Canadian-built Hurricane fighters were already delivered to Britain before the Battle of Britain was decided. One thousand, six hundred and fifty of them were built at Fort William (now Thunder Bay). By 1943 Canada was producing 4000 warplanes a year, and launching a warship a week. Four hundred naval vessels including corvettes, frigates and destroyers, and 393 freighters were launched at Canadian shipyards. In three years the country had become a major industrial nation, and by 1944 was among world's largest producers of war materials.

In 1941 the government took total control of the economy, froze prices, wages and rents, and dicated what goods could be produced. Civilian

OPPOSITE TOP: Building a cargo ship in Canada after World War II.
BOTTOM: The Angus workshops of the Canadian Pacific Railway made tanks during World War II.

ABOVE: D-Day—6 June 1944. Canadian troops going ashore at Bernières-sur-mer, France.
BELOW: Three Canadian war vessels seek out a reported enemy sub in the St Lawrence River.

automobiles, heavy home appliances, tires and inner tubes were no longer manufactured or sold. Gasoline was rationed. Liquor was rationed. Sugar, coffee, tea, butter and meat were rationed.

By the end of that year Canada had landed 124,000 troops in Britain, and 2000 Canadians defending Hong Kong had been killed or captured by the Japanese. There was another Canadian disaster the following year when 5000 were sent ashore at Dieppe to be massacred by the German defences.

Meanwhile the 'corvette navy' was fighting the bitter Battle of the Atlantic, keeping open the supply line to Britain and Russia. In 1941 German U-Boats sank a thousand ships in the Atlantic. In 1942 they sank two thousand.

Halifax was the port where the convoys assembled, St John's a secondary staging port, and one where crippled ships put in for repairs. From there they went north in an arc past Greenland and Iceland, seeking air cover where

possible, escorted by warships that were as yet unable to drive off the submarine packs effectively. For every sub sunk the Germans launched eight new ones. For every freighter launched by the allies, two were being sunk.

In that year the U-Boats moved into the Gulf of St Lawrence, where they sank 23 allied ships, and closed the ports of Quebec and Montreal. They also made two attacks on Bell Island in Newfoundland where freighters loaded iron ore for allied smelters, sank four ships and blew up the pier.

The battle against the U-Boats was won, at last, by increased aircraft cover, and by superior detection devices that finally gave the surface craft the edge. During the long and costly battle, ships of the Royal Canadian Navy escorted 25,000 freighters and troop ships across the Atlantic, and made possible the buildup of troops and war equipment for the invasion of Europe that began 6 June 1944.

The first troops to land on D-Day, as it was

OPPOSITE: A general view of an embarkation scene in Britain as Canadian soldiers left for France during World War II.
ABOVE: Canadian soldiers returning from France.

BELOW: British Prime Minister Winston Churchill visiting Premiere Maurice Duplessie of Quebec, 16 September 1944 was the date of the meeting.

called, were from a Canadian parachute battalion, followed by the 3rd Division and the 2nd Armoured Brigade; 30 thousand Canadians took part in the landing, and, after the Battle of Normandy, went on to capture the channel ports of France and Belgium. The First Canadian Army fought five weeks before Antwerp, then went on to liberate Holland. Other units of the Canadian army fought in North Africa, Sicily and Italy.

When the war in Europe ended with the unconditional surrender of the German army, Canada had three divisions of troops in Europe, a hundred thousand men in the navy, and a quarter of a million in the RCAF. More than a million Canadians had worked in the war industries that converted Canada into one of the leading industrial nations of the world.

The New Day

Newfoundland became Canada's tenth province on 1 April 1949, following a referendum in which a little less than 52 percent of the people voted to join Canada.

Newfoundland had been colonized by European fishermen in the 16th century, settled by both fishermen and 'planters' at about the same time as Nova Scotia and Quebec, had achieved responsible government in 1855, and Dominion status in 1925.

Canada had contested the ownership of Labrador in 1927. Newfoundland's claim to all the land draining into the Labrador Sea was confirmed by the Privy Council, and reconfirmed by Canada in the Terms of Union in 1949. At the date of entry Newfoundland had enjoyed a full decade of great prosperity in her fishing, forest and mining industries, had paid off nearly all of her national debt, and had accumulated a large cash surplus, which was used by the first provincial government for social and economic development.

For Canada, too, it had been a period of great prosperity. There was no post-war recession such as had caused economic and social chaos after the First World War, but a continuing boom that made the nation an economic and political world power.

TOP: Toronto is the most populous city in Canada.
BELOW: The welcoming ceremonies when Newfoundland became a province, 1 April 1949. The photograph taken at the Peace Tower, Ottawa, Ontario shows Prime Minister Louis St Laurent at left next to Viscount Alexander.

The political ties with Great Britain had loosened gradually. During and after the First World War, Canada had struggled to establish her right to fight the war as a separate entity and to follow her own foreign policy. By the end of the Second World War she was not only one of the founding members of the United Nations, but was beginning to follow an anti-imperialist policy contrary to traditional British interests—a policy that made Canada one of the principal mediators between the established Great Powers and the emerging nations of the Third World.

Immediately after the war, Canada began to develop her own nuclear technology, and had established the first experimental reactor at Chalk River, Ontario in 1945. This led to the Candu power generator, using enriched uranium as a fuel, and heavy water as a coolant. By 1980 the Candu was producing one-tenth of

ABOVE: A view of the Trans-Canada Highway, which extends from the Atlantic to the Pacific.
BELOW: The St Lawrence Seaway locks.

Canada's electric energy, and was proclaimed by its sponsors to be the world's safest and most efficient nuclear power system. The claim might be challenged, but in any event the Candu was competing successfully in the international market against quite different systems developed in Great Britain, France, the Soviet Union and the United States.

Oil discovered at Leduc, Alberta set off a new drilling boom in the west. Canada was soon producing more oil than she consumed, and had proven natural gas reserves greater than she could either consume or sell. Canada continued in an oil-surplus position until the early 1970s, when imports again became higher than exports. Drillers then moved into the Arctic, with mixed results, but discoveries on the continental shelf east of Newfoundland and Nova Scotia in 1979 and 1980 made it seem likely that production in that region would equal or exceed that of the Alberta oil fields.

Great petro-chemical industries were established in Alberta and Ontario. Canada became a leading producer of plastics and rare metals, chemicals, fertilizers, and small aircraft, especially types designed for bush flying. Iron ore discoveries in northern Quebec and Labrador opened one of the world's largest iron fields to feed heavy industry in southern Canada and

LEFT: Henri Richard, one of the most prolific scorers in the history of the Montreal Canadians.
BELOW: Barrel racing at the Calgary Stampede. This July event attracts 1 million people.

the northern United States. At Churchill Falls in central Labrador, Newfoundland built the world's largest generating station, transmitting six million horsepower of hydroelectric energy southward to Quebec and the northeastern United States. Quebec followed, about ten years later, with the James Bay development, designed to be an even greater energy producer than Churchill Falls.

In the 1950s and '60s, the Trans-Canada Highway was built through all ten provinces from Victoria, on the Pacific, to St John's, on the Atlantic. Other major highways of four lanes or more were built across southern Ontario and Quebec.

RIGHT: Lester B Pearson (right) with John G. Diefenbaker.
BELOW: Two members of Canada's Queen's Own Rifles, preparing to leave for the Middle East, 1956.
BOTTOM: Soldier on guard.

The St Lawrence Seaway, which could handle only small ships during the Second World War, was expanded during the 1950s so as to bring the largest freighters of the time into the Great Lakes. In addition to creating a direct water route to the industrial heart of the continent, the Seaway produced large amounts of electric energy.

Canada's international status reached a new peak during the 1950s, especially during the Suez Crisis, when, during one of the recurring wars between Israel and her neighboring states, British and French forces occupied the Suez Canal zone, and engaged in some sporadic skirmishing with Egyptian troops.

Canada, acting through the United Nations, succeeded in helping to settle the Suez affair, getting foreign troops off Egyptian soil, and setting up the first United Nations peacekeeping force on the Israeli-Egyptian border. Canada's status in the Third World soared to new heights, and her Secretary of State for External Affairs, Lester Pearson, received the Nobel Peace Prize in 1957.

Canada's status as a third force, and a peace-keeper, did not last. By the time of the Six Day War between Israel, on the one side, and Egypt, Jordan and Syria, on the other (June 1967) Canada was regarded in the Third World as a mere satellite of America.

Efforts to rebuild her international reputation were only slowly successful. That reputation was strengthened when Canada granted diplomatic recognition to the People's Republic of China at a time when the United States was still maintaining the fiction that the legitimate Chinese government was the one in exile on the island of Formosa. Canada refused to accept atomic weapons for continental defense against a hypothetical attack by the Soviet Union. Canadian independence was further strengthened when Canada continued to trade with Cuba despite American efforts to secure a continental embargo against that small communist state (the first lasting communist regime in the Western Hemisphere). Canada also maintained her neutrality during the American war in Vietnam, and granted political asylum to thousands of American war-resisters, deserters, and draft-dodgers, some of whom remained in Canada and became Canadian citizens.

All these efforts to establish an identity and foreign policy separate from that of the United States began to bear fruit in 1980, when Canada's Prime Minister Pierre Elliott Trudeau launched an important initiative to create new links between the 'developed' and 'developing' countries—a 'north-south dialogue' in which Canada would once more act as mediator between the big industrial powers and the economically weaker but often more populous nations of Asia, Africa and South America.

Canada's social development took a major turn with Quebec's 'quiet revolution' of the 1960s. Quebec, up to that time, had been extremely conservative. Her politics had been right-wing. Social and family life was dominated by a Roman Catholic priesthood that was still untouched by the 20th century. Quebec was one of the last places in the democratic world to extend the vote to women—in 1940. Men in Quebec could still be jailed for wearing topless bathing suits in the 1950s. Anyone advocating socialism, birth control, women's

TOP: Olympic Stadium, where the Montreal Expos play baseball.
ABOVE: Downtown Calgary, Alberta.

rights or sexual freedom was likely to be arrested. Even religious freedom was curtailed by the infamous Padlock Law. It was used to silence various minority groups, including the Jewish People's Order of Montreal, until it was finally overthrown by the Jehovah's Witnesses in a long legal battle that ended in the Supreme Court of Canada.

During the 1950s Quebec experienced a great industrial revolution. Because society there was still almost feudal, Canadian and American manufacturing businesses rushed in to take advantage of low wages and unorganized workers. By the end of the decade the province was producing 30 percent of Canada's manufactured goods, but there was a rising tide of

ABOVE: A view of the city of Vancouver, British Columbia.
LEFT: Quebec City.

hatred for the 'Anglo' masters who ran the factories and reaped the profits. The discontent grew into the Quiet Revolution of the 1960s, when Quebec abandoned its love affair with the past in a great wave of unionism, socialist theory, sexual freedom and anticlericism.

At the same time, Quebec woke up to cultural and human rights. The French language ceased to be something one spoke because one had failed to learn English, and became a matter of pride. A true cultural renaissance began—literature, painting, music, theatre. In many arts Quebec led the way toward a true national culture, with English Canada, more than four times larger, laboriously following in her wake.

In the 60s there was a rapid rise of separa-

tism in the province, and the separatists soon had their terrorist wing, carrying out bombings, political kidnappings, and finally the murder of a provincial cabinet minister. The kidnappings were the work of a small band of activists, the *Front de Libération du Québec*. Very few Quebecois, even those who wished for separation from Canada, supported the FLQ. The vast majority of Quebec separatists believed in democratic and peaceful methods. They supported the *Parti Québécois*, a legal organization that proposed to achieve Quebec independence by negotiation with the government of Canada.

When the kidnappings occurred in 1970, the Canadian government reacted with something like panic, declared a state of war emergency, suspended civil liberties, sent the army into Quebec, and loosed a reign of police terror. Hundreds of liberals, union leaders, even feminists, were thrown into jail without charges being brought against them. Few members of the FLQ were caught in this indiscriminate roundup. It was enough to be suspected of separatist sympathies. Eventually, the innocent were all released. The guilty were never arrested. The result was to create, in Quebec, a

greater mistrust of the Canadian government than before, and a greater demand for peaceful separation. In the succeeding provincial election, the *Parti Québécois* formed the official opposition. In the one following (1976) they formed the government.

René Levesque, the separatist leader who came to power that year, was in no hurry to achieve independence for his province. He had promised that no separation would take place without a previous referendum on the subject. Over the next four years he kept modifying his proposal until it emerged as a mandate to negotiate with the federal government on the subject of sovereignty association—a form of semi-independence that would keep Quebec tightly tied to Canada. Even this proposal was decisively defeated by the people of Quebec. In a 60 to 40 percent split they voted to stay in confederation—the largest majority ever recorded in any province that had voted on the issue.

Despite this reverse the *Parti Québécois* was returned with a majority in the next provincial election (1981) giving René Levesque a clear

mandate to continue fighting for special status for Quebec, but inside, not outside, the Canadian union.

The only Canadian leader in recent times with a popularity like Levesque is also from Quebec, and has similar origins—intellectual, populist, leftist, a career beginning in journalism. Pierre Elliott Trudeau, scion of a family that immigrated from France in the 17th century, is as popular among English as among French Canadians. The word 'Trudeaumania' was coined to describe the emotional following he attracted when he entered politics in 1968.

Trudeau's single greatest accomplishment came during his fourteenth year in office (he had been out of power for a brief six months in 1979-80 during a minority Conservative government). Following a prolonged and complex series of negotiations with the premiers of the ten provinces, he achieved a consensus on the constitution that was acceptable to nine premiers, to the federal government, and to all three major political parties in the Canadian Parliament.

Up to this time the Canadian constitution had been the British North America Act, resi-

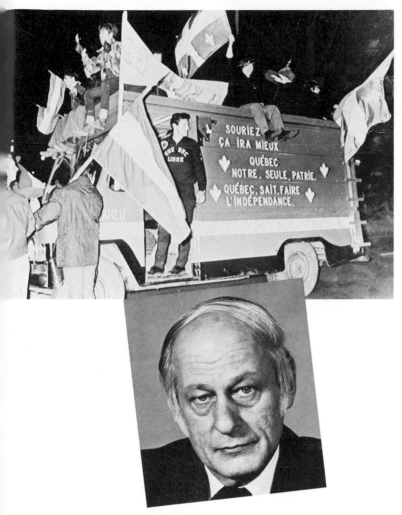

OPPOSITE: French-Canadian separatists greet French President Charles de Gaulle in Quebec, 23 July 1967.
TOP: A photograph taken in October 1969 of Quebec separatists demonstrating for independence in Montreal.
ABOVE: René Levésque, the premiere of Quebec and the separatist leader.

dent in Great Britain, amendable only by the British parliament, and only on petition from the government of Canada. In 1982 the constitution would be brought home with a charter of human rights incorporated, and with an amending formula that would permit the government, with a majority of the provinces and the population, to make changes to it in the future.

In many respects this was the final act of Canadian independence, the last step in a long series that had severed Canada's ties with Great Britain. First the colonies, beginning with Nova Scotia, had been granted representative government. They had united into a federal union presided over by a British governor-general, in 1867. Fifty-two years later they had established an international presence separate from Great Britain by becoming a member of the League of Nations, with a separate foreign policy. Then, in the Second World War, they had fought as an independent nation under the joint Allied command. They had steered an independent course in the United Nations General Assembly that followed, and in the Security Council. In 1952 the Governor-General for the first time was a Canadian, appointed on the advice of the federal government. In 1965 Canada adopted its own maple leaf flag to replace the union jack and variations of it that had flown as a national flag until then. In 1967 *O Canada* was adopted officially as the national anthem, replacing *God Save the Queen*. Like the flag, the new national anthem was equally acceptable in French and English Canada.

That year was the centennial of Confederation, celebrated with many symbolic acts. The Order of Canada was created to honour people who had distinguished themselves in various forms of public service—replacing the British Empire orders and knighthoods that had existed in colonial times. The word 'Royal' was dropped from most Canadian institutions. Expo '67, frequently rated the most successful world's fair in history, drew 20 million visitors to Montreal. At that point all ties with Great Britain had been severed, even the symbolic ones, except for the constitution, which remained in the keeping of the British Government, and the symbolism of the Queen.

The constitution, because it was no mere symbol, but a powerful instrument setting out the limits of authority among the various governments, federal and provincial, and the people whom they ruled, was by far the thorniest issue of the lot. When it was finally settled, late in 1981, the members of all parties stood in their places in the House of Commons in Ottawa and sang *O Canada,* one of the rare occasions when parliament achieved a sense of emotional and intellectual unity.

There would be other crises ahead, perhaps as severe as the separatist crisis of the 1970s, but despite economic and political troubles, the nation had achieved once more a sense of unity and a self-confidence that most Canadians believed would carry them through to new and higher achievements in years to come.

Appendix I

Some Significant Dates in Canadian History

c.1005 AD.	Norse colony established in northern Newfoundland, first European child, Snorri, born in Canada.
1121	Eric, Bishop of Greenland, visits 'Vinland.'
1347	Last recorded Norse voyage to Labrador.
1420	Basque whalers reach Labrador Sea.
1480	Bristol merchants reach western fishing grounds.
1497	Cabot voyage initiates massive international fishery in Newfoundland and Nova Scotia.
1503	Bristol company attempts Newfoundland colony.
1520	Portuguese attempt Cape Breton colony.
1535	Cartier discovers the St Lawrence.
1541	Roberval attempts colony on St Lawrence.
1583	Gilbert takes possession of Newfoundland for England, proclaims first English laws in the New World.
1598	French colony on Sable Island survives five years.
1605	Port Royal founded.
1608	Quebec founded.
1610	Cupids founded.
1613	First recorded birth of English child at Cupids.
1615	Whitbourne appointed Vice-Admiralty Judge in Newfoundland.
1617	Trepassey founded.
1621	Ferryland founded. Scots authorized to colonize Nova Scotia.
1626	First Newfoundland census—320 English families established between Cape Race and Cape Bonavista. Estimated 2000 shore fishermen and 12,000 ship fishermen in 640 vessels.
1628	First conquest of Quebec by David Kirke.
1633	French return to Quebec with first permanent settlers.
1636	Montmagny becomes first governor of New France.
1638	Sir David Kirke becomes first governor of Newfoundland.
1642	Montreal founded.
1649	Hurons wiped out by Iroquois. Jesuits martyred.
1654	English conquest of Acadia.
1666	First census of New France—3215 inhabitants.
1670	Hudson's Bay Company chartered.
1697	D'Iberville raids destroy English settlements in Newfoundland and Hudson's Bay. Settlers return within a year.
1713	Treaty of Utrecht establishes British sovereignty over Hudson's Bay, Newfoundland and Nova Scotia.
1734	La Vérandrye family builds Red River post and explores westward, discovers Rocky Mountains.
1749	British build great naval fortress at Halifax.
1752	*Halifax Gazette* founded. First printing press.
1755	Expulsion of Acadians from Nova Scotia.
1758	Fall of Louisbourg.
1759	Fall of Quebec.
1762	St John's taken by French, recaptured by English.
1774	The Quebec Act.
1775	American attack on Quebec defeated.
1776-1783	Fifty thousand British Empire Loyalists enter Canada.
1785	St John, New Brunswick receives royal charter. New Brunswick separated from Nova Scotia.
1791	Ontario separated from Quebec.
1812	War with the United States. American attempt at conquest fails.
1837	Rebellions in Ontario and Quebec.
1838	Second Quebec rebellion suppressed with great brutality.
1864	Fathers of Confederation meet at Charlottetown, Prince Edward Island.
1867	Ontario, Quebec, New Brunswick and Nova Scotia united into the Canadian confederation.
1869	Rupert's Land purchased from Hudson's Bay Company.
1870	Province of Manitoba created by federal statute.
1871	British Columbia enters confederation.
1873	Prince Edward Island enters confederation.

Edward Richard Schreyer, the Governor General of Canada, and his wife being escorted by Royal Canadian Mounted Policemen to the opening of Parliament. Schreyer was appointed Governor General in 1979.

Pierre Elliott Trudeau, twice Prime Minister of Canada and leader of the Liberal Party. When he returned to power in February 1980, re-elected in a landslide, he had been out of office a mere nine months.

Appendix II
Canadian Prime Ministers

1885	Northwest rebellion defeated. Riel hanged. Canadian Pacific Railway completed.
1898	The Yukon gold rush.
1905	Saskatchewan and Alberta enter confederation.
1914-18	First World War.
1917	Canadian army, united under a single command, takes Vimy Ridge.
1919	Winnipeg general strike.
1930	Great depression. Dust Bowl on Prairies.
1939-45	Second World War.
1940-43	Battle of the Atlantic.
1949	Newfoundland enters confederation
1952	First Canadian-born Governor-General.
1957	Canada helps settle Suez crisis.
1959	St Lawrence seaway opened.
1962	First Canadian satellite launched.
1970	FLQ separatist crisis in Quebec.
1980	Quebec votes to remain in confederation.
1982	Constitution with charter of rights established in Canada.

1867-74	John A Macdonald
1874-78	Alexander Mackenzie
1878-91	John A Macdonald
1891-92	John Abbott
1892-94	John Thompson
1894-96	Mackenzie Bowell
1896	Charles Tupper
1896-1911	Wilfrid Laurier
1912-20	Robert Borden
1920-21	Arthur Meighen
1921-26	William Lyon Mackenzie King
1926	Arthur Meighen
1926-30	William Lyon Mackenzie King
1930-35	R B Bennett
1935-48	William Lyon Mackenzie King
1948-57	Louis St Laurient
1957-63	John Diefenbaker
1963-68	Lester Pearson
1968-79	Pierre Elliott Trudeau
1979-80	Joe Clark
1980	Pierre Elliott Trudeau

INDEX

Picture Credits